"In this fast-paced world we live in, we are tempted to view every circumstance as either an accident or a coincidence, but for those of us who have experienced a comeback, we realize that nothing happens by accident. God has a divine blueprint for each one of us and our painful experiences have a creative purpose. God's divine providence is an amazing reality that you must learn to recognize. Eric has released some fresh revelation in this future best seller!

Furthermore, he is one of the finest preachers in America. He is a Godly husband, father, and pastor, as well. His providential journey is proof that God will take you from nowhere and give you a creative purpose. I'm blessed to be in covenant with this man of God.

I highly recommend "Divine Blueprint" to all who want more out of this life and are ready to be used by God. God uses people that the world can't see coming.

Dr. Ronnie Phillips, Jr., Lead Pastor of Abba's House in Hixson, TN & renowned author of *The Hero Within* (ronniephillips.org).

DIVINE

BLUEPRINT

DIVINE

BLUEPRINT

WHAT THE WORLD CALLS COINCIDENCE GOD CALLS PROVIDENCE.

Eric Clark

GOD GAVE YOU A FINGERPRINT THAT NO ONE ELSE HAS, SO YOU CAN LEAVE AN IMPRINT THAT NO ONE ELSE CAN.

ISBN: 978-0-578-58813-1

DEDICATION

To my children who will hold this book long after I am gone; this will give you the keys to life. Listen to your daddy's heartbeat and don't let your dreams die.

Wherever I get off the train of life, I want you to know who I was.
I love you Jaden, Jude, Presley, Eva (in Heaven), and Jace.

CONTENTS

ACKNOWLEDGMENTS

Thank you:

To Lindsey, my wife, who is the greatest thing (besides Jesus) that I have going in my life!

To my chief editor and biggest supporter, Megan DeWeese, who took this project from an embryonic rough draft and streamlined this work into a life-changing book. This book would not have been possible without you.

To those who have stood with me over the years in ministry, I have moved forward with this project with the strength you have given me through prayer, support, and encouragement.

To Ronnie Phillips Jr., for the love and support!

Lastly, to my Creative Church family who have been faithful to God and my family over the years. I love you.

INTRODUCTION

The book you are holding was done as far as I was concerned. Then, the unthinkable happened. On a cold, winter day, I heard the worst words ever. "Rewrite the book." Like a voice from within, it whispered to me. Everything on the inside of me was ready to be done and release the book. I had labored for 10 long years just trying to write, publish, and release this book and now I knew deep within my heart that I had to start over. Have you ever been in a season where you felt like you were coming to the fourth quarter of and all of the sudden you heard God say, "Go back to the start?" It sounds defeating, but it's actually how we grow and gain wisdom. Sometimes you have to start over. That's life. You may be months or years into your walk with God and hear him say "Start over." If you don't believe God loves new beginnings, consider the sun that rises daily on a fresh course, or the seasons that shift every quarter. God changes the times and seasons. Why would He not be the God of "going back to our first love in Him"? Indeed, He is just that.

I realize that to even think about the phrase "starting over" is frightening for most people. Could the hardest thing and the right thing be the same thing? Imagine going on a cross- country trip from Los Angeles to New York and then realizing that you forgot something. Then, you have to get back in the car and drive back. That's exactly how I felt. So, I made the decision to start over. "Why?", you ask.

After ten years, I felt like so much had changed since the book's inception. Lindsey and I had relocated to a city where we didn't know a soul to go on the adventure of a lifetime. We were about to launch the dream in our heart called Creative Church. We now had five children, instead of two, and had buried a daughter in the process. We had bought a home, almost quit a few times, went through a few pets, and, most-of-all, we had *changed* as people. We were no longer 22-year-old newlyweds. We were in our late-thirties and so much about life had changed!

A part of me was totally hopeless to think I had to start over. Another part of me was thrilled because I knew that something inside of me had changed for the better. **I had aged.** What was lodged in my spirit since I was a child was now ready to be released. I was seasoned now and the battles I had fought had left my soul full of a war fog. Surprisingly, laying in the bottom of my heart was a moist, foggy film. That thin layer of film was the gold dust that I was supposed to start my book over with.

I had now come to the realization that all moments were not created equal. God had delayed the release of this book because of His timing. There was a season that I was going to come to in my life where this book was to be born from. That season had finally come. It was all a part of the plan He had for me. It was all in the blueprint. It was all being burned, processed, and produced inside of me throughout those ten years and I was, for the most part, unaware of it. It was a set of prints, blueprints, that is. The blueprints were now drawn up, written over, torn up, redrawn, and edited in grace over and over again. Now I, as the vessel, was ready to have the contents poured in. The blueprints were ready to be revealed.

CHAPTER ONE

IT'S ONLY MAKE BELIEVE

Something about childhood is magical. When you are a kid, the world is huge, and every dream is possible. Childhood is one-quarter fact and three-quarters fantasy. A new adventure is right around the next corner and the most ordinary thing can become pure entertainment. Childhood is simple and complicated all at the same time. One minute you're having the time of your life and the next minute you are crying hysterically over what, in all reality, is probably no big deal at all. One minute you are fighting with a sibling or friend like two wolves over a meal, and the next minute you've made up and are best friends forever. Having four children in my home always keeps me inside the mind of a child. I wipe tears, change diapers, run out of band-aids, and have Friday night wrestling matches that even my daughter engages in. A child's life is filled with dress-up, imaginary characters, and make-believe. No child should have their childhood taken from them for any reason. As a kid, I loved playing make-believe. Make-believe is the most inexpensive, yet highly entertaining game a child can learn. As a matter-of-fact, let's start a round of it right now.

Let's pretend and make believe that you and I are 20 or 30 years down the road of this life right now. Play along!

What will you look like?
What will be your daily or weekly habits?
Where will you be living?
What will you be doing?
Will you have the same vocation?
What will be the key principles you live by and what will spontaneity look like for you?
Will you be single, married, or divorced?
Will you be a lover, fighter, blamer, bully, or victim?

Have you ever been asked "Where do you see yourself in five or ten years?" People usually respond to this with a safe and predictable answer. It usually sounds like, "I will be happily married, debt-free, and owning my own business."

This can be a reality, but the majority of the time, it's not even close! No one really plans a life with trouble, detours, or heartaches in mind. There is certainly nothing wrong with being positive about our future. I think we all should be optimistic about tomorrow. I know a lot of people that are interested in *what will happen*. Whether their passion is global warming, biblical

14

prophecy, or general spirituality, they want to know about what the future will hold. We should have an interest in the future because that's where we are all going.

IT WON'T BE LIKE THIS FOR LONG

Time is the ever-changing season that we are stuck in. Time is a cruel mistress to us all! Time stops for nothing or no one. Men cry from the streets "time is money", and others yell out across the business halls "you're wasting my time." It seems to be ticking at a more rapid pace than ever before. Technology is evolving every second and our lives are changing at a brisk pace. Life itself brings change. If you are alive, then you will make changes whether you are aware of it or not. Days will turn into weeks. Weeks will turn into months, months turn into years, and hidden from human perception, years have passed. Some situations have turned around and other circumstances have turned upside down.

I remember when I was a little boy, my grandmother would say to me, "Eric, it won't always be this way." As a child, I just couldn't understand what she meant. In my mind "this way" that she referred to seemed like an eternity. In this ever-divided country and world, it seems that the only thing that everyone agrees on is that "time flies." Not only is time flying, but it seems to be flying at a more rapid pace than ever before.

WHO ARE THE JONESES?

Every day, men and women rise and go to work. I've met mothers and fathers who are working themselves to the bone. Why is this? If you were to ask the average parent in America why they are working endless hours, long days, and burning the occupational candle on both ends, they would probably say "To make ends meet." Is that really why? I've heard people make the statement "I wish I had what they have!" I always want to respond with "Do you mean you wish you had their debt?"

The average family in America is living in significant debt.

Why do we do this? The bills we are stacking up are stealing the most prized possession we have. It's called TIME. Are these bills categorized as true needs, or vain wants?

I'm sure you have heard the phrase "keeping up with the Joneses." The phrase is a figure of speech that communicates our deep desire to maintain our social status with those in our circle of life. We work endless hours to keep up with the Joneses. We think we are "getting a piece of the American pie." Yet, in reality, we are drowning in a lack of purpose. We soon discover that the *pie* has poison within its crust. The American dream is like a mirage dancing on the water of our mind. We see a thing. We a see a picture. We see an image. We perceive this to be real. For example, you see an image on Facebook of a handsome man or a beautiful woman and your mind thinks,

"Oh, they look like they have it all together." Have you ever seen someone in a picture and then met them in real life and they look nothing like the image you saw in a fleeting glimpse? We are sold a lie and the lips that sell it have to do very little to make us totally buy it. The lie is simply that a false reality (the reality we want people to think is real) can be attained if we just keep up with the Joneses. Remember, you are looking at a snapshot of others' lives, not the actual reality. **Don't take the bait.**

Have you ever thought, "Who are the Joneses?" No one ever seems to know who they really are nor where they live. We sling a paycheck through the front door only to watch it fly out the back door. We are living stressed, overworked, and spiritually drained.

By the time Sunday morning rolls around, we try to crawl out of the hole of our hectic schedules and visit God's house, that is if we even have the strength to make it there. We find ourselves falling asleep during the service from exhaustion, distractions, or boredom. Are we going into debt to belong to a social group? Seems that way, doesn't it? As a matter of fact, we are selling our birthrights as children of God, by the minute, to win the approval of others or be a part of their crowd.

Esau did this in the book of Genesis. I wonder if he would still trade his divine blueprint for a cheap bowl of soup? Doubtful. Could it be possible that we are striving to find our identity and omitting the Almighty God in that conversation? I think that's where we are in this world. We will give our very souls to be or look relevant. To be irrelevant would be the unpardonable sin. Is this really the plan of God for our lives? Is there a blueprint that we have overlooked all the while building our lives upon the sands of this world? We end up in seasons where we are on the mountain of perspective or trying to make it through the valley. Then, we look back on our life remembering times that were far less complicated. So, where will you be in five, ten, or twenty years?

DREAM AGAIN

Dream big. Dream with your eyes open. God will give you grace to start over if you need to. Maybe you have dreamed a dream only to have that dream shattered and broken in your life. Like Joseph in the Bible, it's time to dream again! If you are breathing, then there is hope. The dream is free. It is the process of that dream that will cost you.

When we are in our late teens, the wheels of the future are turning as we are thinking about what lies ahead of us. What will our college major be, or will we even go to college? Then as we get older, we begin to see the blueprint for our lives as it unravels. So much of life in our twenties is locked down simply because we are not truly seasoned enough to handle certain things. It's like having children. When you have your first child, you are so protective and every second is spent making sure the child doesn't choke or something worse. However, after a few kids, you are not nearly as up-tight and pressurized as a parent.

18

Take the issue of stress as an example. Usually the older someone gets, the more they realize what a waste that worrying actually is. Have you ever cured any problem by worrying? Neither have I! Worrying creates mountains, but faith moves them. Choose faith. It's hard to do this life without a blueprint. It's even harder to try to do this life without Jesus Christ, the Author of your blueprint.

There is such a peace from God that comes upon you as you begin to see your blueprint evolve and unroll. You don't have to wait until you are in your latter years to see God's blueprint. Joseph had a dream from God at the age of 17. This dream revealed to him the blueprint for his life, his nation, and his family. He saw his life unfold before him in high-definition. What God didn't show him was the process of how this dream would come to pass. Usually, this is the way God does things. God gives us a vision. He plants it deep inside of us and causes our passions to flow in the direction of that vision. As our passions draw us toward the vision He gave us, trials will come into our lives to foster the character we need to sustain that vision.

So, what you should be asking by now is "What is meant by the phrase *divine blueprint?*" I'm sure you have heard of the fundamental questions of life. Why am I here? Where did I come from? Where am I going? Why did God allow my mother and father to conceive me? What is my real purpose in the earth? These fundamental questions normally don't get answered until later in life. Often times, the answer comes through a crossroads moment in our life. These fundamental questions aren't really *fun* at all, but they are extremely important for your blueprint to come into full development.

IF YOU LOVE WHAT YOU DO

Traditional education, which is good, teaches us to go to school for twelve years and then off to college for at least four more. It is then that most cross the finish line of education and enter the workforce. Ironically, this is where the real education truly begins. You have heard it said before "if you love what you do, you'll never work again." I think this statement can be somewhat deceptive. We must get out of any reality that does not exist. There is no virtue in ignorance.

God never intended for us to do *nothing*. God has never given anyone an occupational dream and not asked them to mix works with their faith. You don't pray for a harvest, you obey for a harvest. The laws of increase have already been put in place by God. First, no matter what God has called you to do in this life, you will have days when it's just not all you thought it would be. This doesn't mean that you are not called to do great things, even if those great things are grueling things at times. Every crown has a cross to bear. That's called life. God has written a will and blueprint just for you. It had your name on it before you were formed in your mother's womb. Yet, once you truly discover the blueprint that God has written with you in mind, it will change the very principles that you carry to that field, the passion that you bring to the table, and the motivation you will need to continue to reach for the high calling, no matter the cost.

Consider this, if you love what you do, you will work diligently to continue to love what you do. If you feel like you have been divinely called by God and you love your occupation then, by all means, show up and be passionate about it!

ONE BIG, REDEMPTIVE CANVAS

"For we are His **workmanship**, created in Christ Jesus unto good works, which God hath beforehand ordained that we should walk in them." **Ephesians 2:10, King James Version**

What does this scripture mean? The word "workmanship" here has several meanings. Particularly, it refers to us being God's handiwork, fabric, or masterpiece. God has created everyone that is born on this planet and yet, everyone created by God hasn't been redeemed. Redemption only comes through placing our faith in the person and work of Jesus Christ who died for our sins. Those who have this salvation are called the "redeemed." We are literally God's painted canvas. Our lives are broken pieces of canvas by which God is creating His masterpiece. We are broken, but in the hands of the Almighty Artist, we are strokes of blessing. This is truly grace defined. The vessel is marred, but the contents are pure. The frame is damaged, but the image is divine. This is God's grace in its truest form.

God, in all His holiness, is taking broken vessels and allowing us to house His highest treasures of Christ and the grace that comes because of Him. We, as the body of Christ, are one big redemptive canvas that God is ever at work on. You are the canvas and He is the painter. You are the clay and He is the potter. Another way of saying it would be "Believers are pieces to His puzzle." Have you thought about the piece you are designed to play? God doesn't have pieces that do not fit into his puzzle. Yet, rebellion, pride, and self-will will cause your edges to not fit properly. Submit to God if you desire to find your perfect fit.

THE BOLDPRINT

**DON'T FEAR STARTING OVER.
FEAR NOT STARTING AT ALL!**

CHAPTER TWO
STORM RIDERS

It would be difficult to find one thing under the sun that doesn't move in channels of order. Everything in this universe was designed, drawn, and placed strategically by God Himself. This universe is the result of the order of God. Today, the sun came up at God's command. Tonight, the moon will come out and the tides will shift at God's command. Everything around us echoes God's blueprint for the earth. The birds of the air sing His glory and the creatures of the deep are fed by His hand. Every morning God sends the dew to water the earth. No one has to command the dew to fall or evaporate. We don't even think about it. It just happens and yet, without it, the earth would suffer from extreme drought.

AND OUT CAME THE SUN

The Psalmist said:
"The heavens declare the glory of God; and the firmament
sheweth his handywork. Day unto day uttereth speech, and night
unto night sheweth knowledge. There is no speech nor language,
where their voice is not heard. Their line is gone out through all
the earth, and their words to the end of the world. In them hath
he set a tabernacle for the sun, Which is as a bridegroom coming
out his chamber, and rejoiceth as a strong man to run a race. His
going forth is from the end of the heaven, and his circuit unto
the ends of it: and there is nothing hid from the heat thereof."
Psalms 19:1-6, King James Version

I also love another translation of this scripture. The Message
Translation puts it this way:

"God's glory is on tour in the skies, God-craft on exhibit across
the horizon. Madame Day holds classes every morning,
Professor Night lectures each evening. Their words aren't heard,
their voices aren't recorded, But their silence fills the earth:
unspoken truth is spoken everywhere. God makes a huge dome
for the sun-a superdome! The morning sun's a new husband
leaping from his honeymoon bed, The daybreaking sun an
athlete racing to the tape. That's how God's Word vaults across
the skies from sunrise to sunset, Melting ice, scorching deserts,
warming hearts to faith." **Psalms 19:1-6, The Message
Translation**

24

The entire universe is this huge blueprint written up daily by Almighty God. How else can you explain the incredible work of gravity, tides, and the cycles of nature? Take note of how God has placed the sun on a course. If it were to run its "own course", the earth would burn up or freeze. The morning sun comes up like a newlywed husband, the noon day sun beams like an athlete sprinting to the finish line. This is God's clock, His calendar, His blueprint. All around us, there are divine blueprints being drawn out.

How does the deer know to come to the water?
How does the ocean know where to stop its swell?
How do the stars never fade?

They are all on the clock, the calendar, and the blueprint of God.

We are created in the image of God. Just as the sun above our head, we are designed to run the course God has so designed for us. Life becomes a repetitive cycle of defeat when we do not understand that everything God has made has a divine purpose within it. We are the glory that Jesus died for. We are His body on Earth and His bride in Heaven.

If the sun, the moon, and the entire universe reflects God's revealed blueprint, then imagine what God has drawn up for us! We are His highest creation! We are His image!

HEARING ECHOES

Picture yourself ten years down the road of life. What do you see coming? Do you see your life on pace with the will of God? I heard the story of a young man who was hiking with his father. The young man slipped and fell. He was hanging by a tree limb and began to cry out for help. "Daddy, help me," he shouted! He heard a voice come back, "Daddy, help me!" He screamed out, "Who is that?" The voice replied, "Who is that?" The young boy said, "You're stupid!" The voice replied, "You're stupid!" The young boy said, "You're a coward!" and the voice responded, "You're a coward!" The father rescued the boy and the boy said, "Daddy, who was that?" The father replied, "Son, that voice is called *life* and what you put out comes back to you."

The father said, "Let me show you something," and then shouted, "You're a winner!" The echo responded, "You're a winner!"

Are you sending out faith signals to your future? Are you leaning on *your plans* to get you to where God wants you to be? **Your plan will not work.** You can try it. At some point, you will most likely despise your plan. It's a great feeling down deep in your soul to let go of your plans and embrace God's plan. Now, God isn't going to create the future for you. That's your job. God has placed a law into our stewardship of time called sowing and reaping. Each day we are making decisions that will become the very quality of our life in days to come. Positive

26

thinking isn't always Christian, but Christian thinking is always positive! What will your echo say? Will you speak faith, or will you speak fear? Start sending out signals of faith!

HOW DID I END UP HERE?

Have you ever asked yourself, "How did I get to this point in my life?"

It's a fair question. Examination is a scary thing, but often times it's required in order for us to get to a place of wholeness in our lives. If you are one of those people that have it all figured out in life, you can stop reading this book. Most people who live a little come to the end of themselves at some point. It's a beautiful thing to run out of all the answers and find your yourself in total surrender to God.

It's wise to take inventory. Often times, we pray for God to give us wisdom and yet we fear correction. Don't pray for wisdom if you're scared of correction. When we fail to take inventory and receive correction, we end up in emotional, relational, and spiritual bankruptcy.

Elijah is a powerful figure in Biblical history. He appears on the mountain we call Transfiguration in the New Testament, and he even ministers to Christ before His crucifixion. He has the power to bring miracles to pass and even stop the rain from falling from the sky. He comes on the scene as God's law

27

enforcement agent. He stands on top of a mountain and slays 450 prophets of the false god, Baal. His victories are so numerous that in the eyes of many, he is a prophet that cannot fail. The wicked King Ahab and his wife get the word concerning Elijah's victory on Mount Carmel. At this point, they put a death sentence upon the head of Elijah. Elijah hears of this warrant for his life and runs into the wilderness to flee for his life. He goes a day's journey into the wilderness and sits down under a juniper tree. He then will do something that no one would've ever dreamed he would do. He will ask God to take his life. Elijah, the great prophet of God, just wants to end it all.

How can this be? What a change of scenery from one chapter of the Bible to the next. He doesn't look like God's law enforcement agent anymore. He's running like a scared rabbit. It is here in Elijah's cave of discouragement that God will ask him a question. "Elijah, what are you doing here?" In other words, "How have you come to this place in life?" It's like God was saying, "Is this what I planned for you, Elijah?" I can relate to Elijah. God has asked me this same question.

Have you been here in life before? Goodness, I know I have! In the morning, I had the confidence that only the grace of God can bring. I felt victory over self, sin, and the enemy. Then, it would seem that by evening I couldn't even get a grasp on my own life. Have you ever felt this way? One morning, it seems that you have hope and promise running through your veins, and then as the sun is going down, you just want to go down with it.

God doesn't ask any of us a question to obtain information that He doesn't already have. God can't be taken off His guard by anything! God will ask us questions so that we can begin, with steps of honesty, to move in His direction. These steps usually start with true repentance.

Elijah played the blame game and attributed his current situation to the fact that he felt like he was the only one doing anything right in the nation. Haven't we all thrown the same pity party? Maybe we don't express the blame verbally, but deep inside we just want to feel sorry for ourselves as if we are the only ones experiencing certain emotions. Elijah's perspective of this situation was wrong. God had a remnant of 7,000 people that were wholly devoted to Him. Remember, Elijah didn't *see* these 7,000 prayer warrior prophets, so he made the deadly assumption that he was God's only option.

Sometimes, we just need to be honest with God about our current condition. It's really hard to stay fake all the time. It can get very costly to live in dishonesty about our real condition in this life. Have you ever come to this point in life? When you do, don't go into the cave of isolation, but rather learn to be honest with God. Honesty usually leads us to conflict. Yet, in this conflict, we will find true peace if we surrender to God. Once that happens, true wholeness and intimacy can return to our lives.

Elijah walked out of that cave of discouragement, depression, or whatever you'd like to call it, with victory! This victory isn't just for him, but for you as well. You know what was about to happen to this man? He would leave this cave in the power of God and go on a brand-new adventure. What seemed to be the end of his life turned into a brand-new day for him. He would receive a fresh copy, so to speak, of his blueprint. The prophet was back from the dead, emotionally and spiritually. He walked out of that cave and outran everyone, on foot, to anoint a new king and a new prophet named Elisha, who would be his successor. Like Elijah, you can complete the blueprint for your life if you are honest in the hard times. Don't blame others. There's no victory in blame.

NOT LOSERS, BUT CHOOSERS

Many times, our present circumstance in life is not entirely altogether our fault. Yes, I realize that we live in a society where no one seems to take responsibility for anything they do. Honesty is a very rare thing in the times that we live. It's almost as if culture is distinctively training people to cover up, hide, or altogether lie about who we really are. Yet, we all come from different environments and parental styles. Right now, in your life, there are people making choices that positively or negatively affect you. What can you do about this? The answer is nothing. There is nothing you can do to change other people.

You can pray for God to change them, but you are limited to

what you can do. You are never responsible for the decisions that others make. What could you have done about the way you came into this world? We are not born with a choice of who our parents are or who our family will be. These are choices we don't get to make. Yet, there's something much more powerful than human DNA. We are not born winners or losers…we are all born choosers! At some level, you are who you are because of *your* choices and decisions. There are other factors involved in our life that go into this equation as well, but a huge part of our blueprint is the choices we have made or are making.

Now, don't lose hope yet! God's grace enables us to rise from wrong choices and, by His mercy, we can move forward. Forward is the direction God desires for us to go. Remember, honesty leads to conflict but if we are open about our mistakes, this will lead us back to health. God designed us for true intimacy with Him, with family, and with every other relationship as well. We don't have to hide from anyone. *We don't have to feel like we are always out of place.* If you are in Christ Jesus, then you are in your place. Your position has been secured. You may still struggle in a condition that seems to be never-changing but stand up in the grace of God and boldly begin to live for His glory. This isn't a license to sin, but rather a freedom to live holy *in grace.*

THE BLOOD WAS THE INK

We will never come to embrace who we are if we can't forget

who we were. In Christ, I am accepted. I am God's child! I am hidden with Christ in God! I am significant! I am God's workmanship (Ephesians 1:5, Colossians 3:3, Ephesians 2:10). The blood of Jesus was the ink that signed the check to pay for our freedom.

The choices we make today tend to shape the road that takes us to tomorrow. Time works its elusive magic outside of the realm of human perception. Time simply slips by. It seems as though, before long, days turn into weeks, weeks into months, and months into years. Time is just gone! The choices we are making, or have made, begin to really harden into deadly habits. These habits become the cement to the foundation that we build our lives upon. God didn't create us in the image of a helpless puppet. We have the God-given ability to make choices. Let's put to rest this "I can't help it" mentality. Today is a gift. Yesterday is history. Tomorrow, if it comes, is a brand-new canvas. Yesterday is like a cancelled check, tomorrow is a promissory note, but today is cash in hand. Live today!

LEARN FROM EGYPT BUT DON'T LIVE THERE

Many people feel as if they cannot outlive their past. You can't outlive your past trying to be your own spiritual lawyer and savior. You cannot redeem yourself. Yet, if Jesus Christ is the Lord of our life, the past is forgiven and not to be discussed. We are to *learn* from Egypt but not *live* in Egypt! The fact that you are alive right now means that God is not done with your life.

You have had innumerable opportunities to give up and you didn't. Along the journey, you have climbed mountains, walked through valleys, crossed rivers, and marched through deserts.

I'm sure that there's been some bloody wars you've fought along this road called life. Yet, this life is so precious and short. Stop wasting your life by living in regret of what you would have done differently. Regret is the tool of conspiracy that the enemy uses to rob us of the present moment. We can't ever live and enjoy the moment because our minds are always thinking about yesterday. You may not feel as though you can enjoy anything. Don't sink in the quicksand of feelings. What you *feel* won't change anything! Faith moves God. Have faith in God and move forward. Make a move! It may change everything. Staying the same isn't the answer. Change comes into our life either through obedience or pain. Move on.

OPPORTUNITY DRESSES UP

I live on the coast of South Carolina. In the fall of 2016, we endured Hurricane Matthew. Where we live, there was significant damage to the area, thousands of trees were uprooted and blown over by the wind and rain. We had to evacuate along with millions of others and head to higher ground. It was a whirlwind of having to simply find a place to stay and just driving randomly throughout the countryside until we were given the clearance that we could return home. When meteorologists began to scramble trying to predict exactly where the storm would hit, I noticed that as millions of people were running away from the storm, others were running to it! Surfers and thrill seekers were running to the water to be challenged by the storm. Men who owned large heavy-duty equipment such as bucket trucks and chainsaws were moving into the area like swarms of bees. Literally, crews and individuals were making up to $10,000 a week cutting and removing storm debris. For months, I received cards in the mail from people wanting to do storm work.

What millions ran from, others ran to! This is exactly what the present opportunity in your life is like. If you run from every challenge that life brings, you will never fulfill the blueprint for your life. Could it be that the language that we have learned is a language of defeat? For example, we call a job...work. We call delay... denial. We call not having an internet signal... a bad circumstance. I think of our grandparents' generation who worked from sunup until sundown. They were not a generation of complainers, but they were individuals who built their lives around the truth of God, family, and home. Could it be that you have been running from what God has placed in front of you? Embrace obstacles. When what is ahead of you is God's will, then it will be worth the time, sweat, and effort you put forth to see it come to pass.

In this life, I see people sitting back, waiting in the wings for their opportunity to hit them in the head. An opportunity is often veiled and hidden within an obstacle. If you do not discern, perceive, and capitalize on an opportunity, you will miss it. Opportunity is a matter of perception. Opportunity doesn't walk up to you and say "Hello, I am opportunity!" Opportunities are so veiled that they often come in the form of opposition and resistance. You can be gifted, talented, and still live in poverty. In fact, nothing is more common than unsuccessful people with talent. You can be the most intelligent person in the world, but if you cannot discern that your trouble is a training ground for wisdom to develop a perfect work within you, then you will never grow. Growth comes from the dirt of life. **So, what is your dream?**

Please, don't tell me that your dream is what you are living in, driving around, or wearing on your body. The dreams that God gives us are designed to outlive us. These dreams are not limited to the realm of time, supply, or circumstance. God gives us dreams that we don't fully understand. It's only when we get outside of ourselves that we begin to see the reality of what God has for us. We must see ourselves connected to *His plan*, not *our own thing*. Dream big. Dream as big as you want. The dream is free. It's the process of the dream that will cost you.

THE BOLDPRINT

> ### DON'T RUN FROM THE STORM.
> ### IT'S RAINING WITH OPPORTUNITY!

CHAPTER THREE
ONE SHOT

For thousands of years, people have searched for answers to this life and its mysteries. Nothing has changed. We still pursue intelligence as if it is our savior. We look to other people for answers that we don't have. We observe, read, and study to find any elusive golden nugget that may be able to cure our problems. We are being fed, literally, 24 hours daily with media waves of information whether it be true or false. If we don't know something, we simply google it. Be encouraged because there is one greater than google that is here! The hope of the good news of the gospel of Jesus Christ provides for us all the treasures of wisdom and knowledge we will need while here on Earth. Every answer we diligently search for is found in Jesus Christ!

Nevertheless, in our culture, we are constantly trained to *look in*. The free press and media push and pry to lead us down the road of finding our destiny. Such topics as, planning, goals, weight loss, and right attitudes are a huge sale. Now, before you throw me out the door, I understand that not everything that we read or see is altogether unprofitable. There are tons of *good* books and positive thinking outlets among us. There is a difference though. As I said earlier, positive thinking isn't always Christian, but Christian thinking is always positive. God's direction for our life is always *up*. Yet, we are looking *in* for answers. That's a mistake.

Why are these topics such a huge hit on the sale rack? The answer is quite simple: *we don't want to fail.* This, alone, is not necessarily an evil thing. No one wants to fail. Yet, here's the problem: God's way to win is to lose yourself in order that you may find yourself. The world's way shouts, "find yourself" and ultimately, you lose your soul. God's way whispers, "lose yourself" and ultimately, you'll save your soul. God always takes us out of Egypt before He shows us the full plan. He won't give you the good news without the bad news. He won't give you the bad news without giving you the good news either.

I personally believe that we are much more occupationally driven to compete than those who have come before us. They did not have an avalanche of social media and a 24-hour open signal to see what the entire world was doing. What a thought! The enemy, I'm sure, used other means to cause distractions or comparisons, but at least you had to walk down the road a little to find the temptation to look at others and compare.
You may have heard it said, "God has a plan for your life." I remember hearing that for so many years thinking, "I already

have a plan." We can't discover our path in God until we understand our position in God. What's our position? We are lost and damned without Jesus. This is our former position. Our path and plan must start with coming to God in surrender, not in our own success. When we surrender to God and yield to His plan for us, we quickly discover the futility of our own plan. This will lead us to lasting biblical success!

I believe at some point in our lives, a real lack of purpose usually creeps in and we begin to wonder if the *plan* we chose was the right plan. Some people wait until their body breaks down, mind goes drifting, and eyes are dim before they begin to think about eternal purpose.

So, let's ask the question "What is God's will for my life?" If you have put your faith in Jesus Christ, the Bible calls you "righteous." After this, God is not just Creator God, He is now your Father. The world teaches us that it's all about *who* you are. I say it's more about *whose* you are. Whether you are saved or lost, God's will for your life is simple: to shape you into the image of His Son- Jesus Christ. He does this through grace, mercy, and the blood of the Lamb of God, Jesus Christ. He molds us continually and our growth in Him is a daily process. Here's the good news: His grace is MORE than sufficient!

Now, from this plumb line of truth, what will you do? Will you just stand with a sign out on the main intersection of town that reads "I'm just out here bringing God glory"? Of course not! God's spiritual will for you is to be saved, but that is not all.

God desires for us to discover our color in His coat, the piece in His puzzle, and be shaped into the image that He has in mind for His plan.

There are three things we need to make us content. The first is someone to love. So how can we love unless we've been loved? How can we be loved without knowing the love of God-from whom true love springs? Secondly, we need something to do. This is where the piece to the puzzle hits us occupationally and in the area of our passions. You have passions, whether you have discovered them or not, that are in place for the glory of God. Meaningful work is God's way of revealing virtuous principles that shape us. On our job, we learn patience, team work, and discernment among many other things. If you want to learn about structure, then get a job. You'll most likely find order and structure very quickly. I've met people who had no idea what the real world was like until they went into the workforce. Lastly, we need something to look forward to. We are so interested in tomorrow because that's what's coming… if it's God's will.

A DEADLY MISTAKE

We make a deadly mistake in an effort to find the divine blueprint for our life. The mistake is simply that *we look within.* This is a concept from the world. It comes from a culture that says "You, yourself, are the answer."

The Word of God shows us that Jesus is the answer. Instead of looking inside of ourselves, we must lift our head toward the heavens and look up. Look *up* into the face of your creator. It is in Him that you are going to see the blueprint. This blueprint will be full of color, exciting, and will connect the lines in your life. You are not going to find the blueprint from the Lord to be full of lies, disappointment, and monotony. Follow the lines on the blueprint. They will lead you toward the plan!

When a home builder constructs a home, will he just do it at random with spontaneity and have no sequence of order? No, but rather he will research, take notes, jot down ideas, then cut and paste until he has come up with exactly what he wants to see constructed. He draws up the blueprints in an effort to construct physically with material what he is looking at on the plans. In the same way, if you follow your own way, you'll end up with a spiritual and relational house that will crumble when the winds of adversity blow. Follow the lines on the blueprint and you won't live with regrets.

We are getting older. Everyone is. Degeneration is a part of life. We begin to die the moment we are born. You are alive right now. You're not promised tomorrow. You may have to sit down and intentionally allow the Holy Spirit to critically, yet lovingly, examine your life. Listen and obey the Holy Spirit. God will redeem the time and He will begin to set your life in order. God doesn't just see the current perspective alone. God sees the beginning, the end, and all points in the middle. First things first: look up for answers. Then, and only then, can you look inside and make sense of this thing called life. Here is God's order: look up to Him, look inside of yourself, and look out into the world of possibility.

ONE SHOT

I remember being in Hampton, Virginia walking out of my hotel room into the morning sun. I was in my early twenties. I had developed a habit of getting up and going for a jog to set my mind for the day. This day was different in that it seemed as though God was giving me something. It seemed as though I could almost hear God speak to me in an audible voice, though I physically heard nothing. This is a summation of what I heard:

"You have been given one life to live. You are young right now. Life is like a vapor that the sun crashes upon in the morning and suddenly it's gone. Time will fly by. You will blink your eyes and you'll be older. Every action, word, and thought are a seed you are sowing toward tomorrow. I have set eternity in your heart. You have one shot."

It seemed that day that God stopped me in my tracks and spoke deep into my heart. It was in that moment that I received His eternal perspective on my life. This *God-View* of life came sweeping violently into my heart, mind, and soul. This *God-View* is the comprehensive view that God alone sees. God sees yesterday, today, and tomorrow. God is eternal and yet is so personal that He knows the current number of hairs on our head. God sees the entirety of your life.

I remember that day vividly and it seemed like I had this brief cinematic moment in God's presence where, like a Father, He took me up into His arms. Woah! The view was majestic! I could see ahead, it seemed, into the future. I could see everything that was behind me. There I was as a small child, spared, for a reason. I literally could feel so many seasons converging in that moment. It was as if time was being mixed in a blender. It was here that the words *divine blueprint* raced into my mind and I began to write what I was feeling in that moment. It was a wonderful feeling but sobering at the same time. I walked in the strength of that experience for quite some time. Years later, the seed would find the soil and bring to birth the pieces of this book.

PLAN ON PURPOSE

Do people trip into the will of God? Does the will of God just find us on accident or through fleshly pursuit? I say neither. I believe that it takes real concentrated effort in prayer to find the will of God. Once you find the will of God, be bold and submit to it. Submission is the lost art of the church. Don't allow the "quick-fix" culture mindset to get its grip so tight on you that you begin to believe that it doesn't take deliberate effort to be where God wants you to be in life. What is going to happen in your favor without your involvement? The answer is…not much.

Now, understand that ultimately nothing of any eternal worth is going to happen to you without the involvement of God. You are natural and God is super. Him placing His hand upon you is what brings your life into the realm of the supernatural. We aren't going to just drift into success, nor show up in Heaven by random selection. Real living happens on purpose. Think about it!

We take time, energy, and effort to search for the right plan of action when it comes to taking a vacation, going to college, or who we will give ourselves to in marriage. Most people will plan their vacation months or even years in advance. Some even plan down to the hour what they will be doing the entire trip. When we go to college, we visit different schools, write letters, and check out different cities to determine where we will attend. Think about marriage. We date, we court, and we date some more until we have found a person that we believe is *the one.* These are vital decisions. Decisions, like these, effect everything in our life. They influence our children, shape our views of others, and ultimately create the person we will be. How much more time, energy, and focus should we expend searching out the blueprint of God?

The average person goes to college and gets a degree. Then, they jump headfirst into life. Sometimes, the vocational field we are in has very little or nothing to do with our educational degree. Often, through the providence of God, people end up doing a job that they love but had no previous plans of taking. Other times people can be in a vocation that they have a degree for but soon discover they have no real passion toward the actual job. Some even despise it. You've seen both situations, I'm sure. As our career is being launched, at some point, we decide we don't want to rent anymore, and we purchase a home. Decisions such as these, from college choice, occupation choice, and home buying options are extremely important. Yet, the degree can be revoked or suspended, the career destroyed through an unethical decision, and the home can go up or down in flames. In a moment, a lot can change.

Remember when you were in high school? You looked across the field and saw hundreds graduating alongside you, never realizing how the very next morning, or soon after, life would change forever. I think of my graduating class and the students from that class literally live around the world. Everything can change in a blink of an eye. Life itself confirms that this is true. So, what real thought goes into the real will of God for your life? How much have you invested in inquiring with God if you are doing the real will of God for your life? It's a sobering question. Everyone is called. Everyone is called to be a shining light in this dark world.

The farmer wakes up every morning living by the laws of agriculture. He rises before the sun comes up. He plows the ground, plants the seeds, and plucks the weeds. If he does not plan on purpose, his family and his community will go hungry. The farmer is counting on the fact that God will let the sun come up and the rain fall. Farmers don't grow crops, they plant seeds. Sunlight and rain will be the key ingredients to bring the farmers plan to fruition. Yet, the farmer doesn't wait for sun and rain to plow and plant the seed. He's confident in the plan.

I DO THIS FOR A LOVING

Often, I have witnessed people, whether they were a believer in Jesus or not, actually be used by God to accomplish pieces of His will and purpose on this earth. I have also met people who distinctively feel as though their vocation and spiritual calling were one and the same. I hear people say things like "This is what I do for a living (to make money), but such and such is my real passion." I believe that there are things you do for a *living* and there are things you do for a *loving*. When Jesus called twelve men to follow him, they were not unemployed people. If they were fishermen, I'm sure they still fished from time to time. As a matter of fact, Jesus went with them fishing on more than one occasion.

What changed?

When Jesus got into their vocational field, the fish began to fill their nets in such abundance that their nets broke. Now, they were no longer fishing for their family, but they were gathering more than enough food to feed a community. Not everyone is called to stand behind some glass stained window and be a preacher. Our lives preach for us. From the farmer, doctor, firefighter, teacher, or preacher, we all have been held under obligation to find the will of God for our private life and public vocation. Our families are counting on it.

How many people do you currently know that are going into ministry as a vocation? The numbers are not overwhelming. Maybe you see a big crop of people that are just dying to be scrutinized by the public for every mistake they make, but most of the people who begin down the road of ministry never make it to their first assignment. Honestly, ministry is a dying vocation. The Apostle Paul spoke about the "high calling" in Philippians.

"I press toward the mark for the prize of ***the high calling of God*** in Christ Jesus." **Philippians 3:14, King James Version**

Paul wasn't speaking here of what we normally think of as a "high calling". We normally think of people in the vocation of ministry when we hear such phrases. Yet, the occupational attraction of ministry is at an all-time low. The "high call" certainly, for most, isn't the desirable call. In America, we are deceived and blinded to what real success is. We live in an image-driven culture obsessed with making it to "the big time." Often when we arrive at "the big time" it turns out to be not-so-good of a time. We have been sold a lie and we will continue to buy this lie until we come to full surrender in Christ. Money becomes the hinge on which we make our vocational decisions. We rarely follow our divine calling or our passion…usually we follow the money.

CALLED TO STARVE

When money is the dominant motive for why we do what we do, it creates a chasm in our soul that only more money can fill. The only issue with that is that greed never gets a full stomach. It will continue to eat until you are the one consumed. Look around. Nearly everything you read or see is driven by money. People are buying the lie and that's why these companies, media, or businesses that we often condemn are still in business. We keep buying it. We create our own monsters and then ask them to leave. We are sold the lie that being somebody means that you must have the approval of men, fame for a friend, and lots of money. This lie gets into the heart of people whom God is directly calling into ministry. They begin to think "Well if I do this or that (ministry), I'll starve to death!"

Who wants to feel like they have been *called* to starve to death? No one that I know of, at least. We have financial goals that are set by the world's standards. Then, if we don't meet these goals, we assume that this *calling* can't be of God. No one wants to have less, not even me. However, when I am drawing out the plans of what matters most to me in life, I must ask God to trace the plumb line of my life. If that means I take less to accomplish more, then so be it. Put the pen in God's hands and let Him draw out the plans.

I remember when I first felt called to ministry, I worked other jobs to help supplement myself. I remember making less than $15,000 or $20,000 annually for a few years. Was I less blessed? Absolutely not! I was just as loved by God then as I am now. Currently, I am nearly twenty years into the ministry and my salary is more, but my motive is the same. Ministry is about God and loving people. We don't work for God, we work WITH Him. One of my side goals is to live off writing books and itinerant income and not take one dime from my church. I want to be able to do what I do for a loving, not a living!

MONEY, MONEY, MONEY...MONEY

Money isn't evil.

"For *the love of money* is the root of all evil: which while some coveted after, they have erred from the faith, and pierced themselves through with many sorrows." **I Timothy 6:10, King James Version**

Money is NOT evil. It becomes evil when it becomes the god of your heart. How do we know this has happened? It has happened when money gets in your heart, spirit, and mind and it's all you think about. Notice in the previous scripture what follows greed is erring from the faith. Then, notice what comes next is that we end up getting stabbed by the blade of greed. Think about the number of people who became wealthy only to go through great sorrow that followed because they hastened after *other* gods.

Scripture doesn't say "money is evil." Money is like oxygen, it's necessary. However, you don't look at the twelve men that followed Jesus and see them leave their main livelihood to follow Jesus out of pure convenience. Can you hear Peter or John ask Jesus, "Hey Jesus, can we talk about 401k plans, health insurance, and annual salary before we fully commit?" This is funny but probably not the case. These twelve men who were called to follow Jesus didn't move in their heart toward Christ from the basis of convenience, but rather conviction. Something in their heart moved and quickened them at such a level that they were willing to chase their destiny.

STAY OFF THE ROOF

The most dangerous time in a person's life is in the prosperous times. For example, in David's life "at the time when kings go forth to battle," David stayed home. Oh no!

He, for whatever reason, decided he didn't have to engage in battle anymore. The great warrior David was supposed to be in battle. It was battle season. Instead, David got up from his bed and walked out on the roof. Oh no!

David, whom God had allowed to kill sheep-stealing lions and bears. David, whom God had given the head of Goliath to. That David had decided he wasn't going to be a warrior that day. He didn't want to fight. Now, God wasn't looking for David to *defend Him*, and God isn't looking for you to defend Him. He simply wanted David to *represent Him*. The same is true for you.

When David failed to go into battle and be among his soldiers, he got bored and his mind went drifting. His failure started right there! He failed to be with his brothers in battle. He was a worshipper and a warrior a long time before he was ever a big shot king. He had committed the tragic sin of forgetting where he had come from.

This type of passivity is a common thing among men. It is dangerous. Men are called to be on the battle field of life for their family. God will assign seasons of rest and when those seasons come, we need to rest. Yet, men are born to conquer. Had King David stayed in the circle of men, young and old, that God put in his life he would have never been alone and set up for disaster. His sin and lifetime of pain began when he simply *didn't stay with his men*. David had put down his harp of worship, his battle armor, and had picked up a bucket of passivity.

Prosperous times lead to passive wills. Passive wills lead to overpowering emotions. Overpowering emotions lead to impure thoughts. Impure thoughts lead to private sin. And private sin leads to public consequences.

God's blueprint for your life cannot be overvalued. You get the privilege of living and dying in the will of God. It doesn't matter *what* you do, if you don't do what you *should* do! There are three things that seem to kill people: bad decisions, terrible diets, and a lack of dreams. God has designed this blueprint for you. The blueprint is yours to run with or ruin. The package will be delivered to you, but you have to be spiritually home to receive it. God won't simply drop off your blueprint and walk away. Untold millions have decided to be absent when God was giving out blueprints. Others have received the blueprints for their life but have never unrolled the plans. What's the result? Quite simply, we never build anything of eternal value. That is a shame. Get off the roof of exhaustion or boredom and open the blueprint God has patterned for you. It's worth it.

THE BOLDPRINT

> **IT DOESN'T MATTER WHAT YOU DO,**
> **IF YOU DON'T DO WHAT YOU**
> **SHOULD DO!**

CHAPTER FOUR
DNA

"Thine eyes did see my substance, yet being unperfect; and in thy book all my members were written, which in continuance were fashioned, when as yet there were none of them." **Psalms 139:16, King James Version**

This scripture makes me think of **DNA.** Deoxyribonucleic acid can be expressed as a written language that creates a blueprint that makes you who you are. Geneticists tell us that trillions upon trillions of combinations make up human DNA; yet, your unique DNA was formed at the time of conception. You were your own human being, not just from birth, but from day one of conception. Consider that no two human beings have ever come into the world with the exact same DNA. Even in the case of same sex siblings, such as twins, the odds are so small that it's nearly impossible. DNA, in my opinion, gives you incredible proof of God's existence. God, in all His infinite wisdom placed a genetic code inside the human zygote that tells you what you will look like, what your features will be, and even the behavioral characteristics of who you will be. Your mother and father gave you your natural existence. Their physical union brought you into this world.

DNA is so incredibly powerful that it has brought criminal cases to light that would have never been solved without it; and simultaneously, it has acquitted and exonerated many who were falsely convicted and placed into prison. Just like in the human realm there is a genetic code, such is the case in the spiritual realm. Just as your physical DNA tells us what you will look like and what your features will be, your spiritual blueprint gives us clues to your godly assignment. **God gave you a fingerprint that no one else has, so you could leave an imprint that no one else can.**

DRESS REHEARSAL

Your DNA sequence, if written out, would fill up about 1200 encyclopedia volumes. IF that's not impressive, then get this: that same entire DNA sequence can be found in nearly every cell of your body! That means there is enough information inside of you right now to fill every book in the Library of Congress (that is about 35 million books). Everything about you is known by your creator, the God of the Bible! His eyes saw your very substance before you were born, and nothing can be hidden from Him. You were not an accident then, and you are not an accident now. You were placed on this earth for a purpose. I believe that the highest call for every human being is to be conformed to the image of Christ. God is in the business of bringing Christ to perfect light inside the heart of everyone who walks with Him. Jesus, Himself, is the prize of the high call. In eternity, He will be our reward. In eternity, the entire blueprint will be unveiled. The canvas will be fully redeemed and all of God's pieces will be on display. In Heaven, Christ will be the center of all of our worship and affection.

The real meaning of life is to win Christ. However, my destination may be Heaven, but God's destination is my maturity in Christ while on this earth. God is shaping us through His glorious grace into the image of His Son. In Christ, we are perfect and are being perfected. It does not mean that we are without sin. God is not looking at your own righteousness. He is looking at the righteousness of Christ. I hear people reference the scriptures and say, "God is coming back after a bride without spot and blemish." I agree. Yet, the reason the bride of Christ is without spot or blemish is not because she has prepared herself independently of the Holy Spirit. The bride is spotless because she is covered by the righteous robes of her groom-Jesus Christ.

In ourselves, we are full of failure and bound for judgement. A life of self is a life of death. God wants His will to be accomplished in our life before Heaven comes. This life is dress rehearsal for the next one. God's desire is to see you live out your divine blueprint and run your course while you are upon this earth.

So, why even get a job, start a family, or plan and prepare if the entirety of the will of God is just to conform to the image of His Son? Well, you can stand on the side of the road with a sign that reads "I'm just conforming to the will of God, anything will help." However, most people are going to stare at you strangely due to the fact that this goes against all human and spiritual logic. The Bible points us toward meaningful work. We aren't just called to pursue a career, but rather we are called into service for God regardless of the field of life, ministry, or area of employment.

FROM MILLIONS TO MISSIONS

I know of a young woman named Tammy. She graduated from an ivy league college and was in the process of accepting a high-ranking position with a company that is a worldwide player in the realm of technology. Her salary was going to be well over $100,000 annually. It was such a rewarding season for Tammy. She had worked so hard through high school and college and graduated near the top of her class. Her parents had made great financial sacrifice to see their daughter succeed. The thrill of walking across the stage with honors was incredible. The future lay before her and it was as bright as the noon day sun. Her dreams were coming true.

The week before she began her executive job, she was to fly back home for one final, quick visit. That Sunday while attending the church that she grew up in, something happened to her that she could have never predicted. Tammy had an encounter with God. That Sunday, an evangelist spoke to the congregation. It was the same evangelist that had preached many years ago when she was just a young girl. Tammy remembered being that little girl.

The evangelist was a missionary. This particular Sunday, he showed videos, pictures, and told the story of his missions. There on the screen were young girls that were starved, raped, and trafficked for sex. Tammy's heart was moved with a penetrating awareness of sorrow and conviction.

For Tammy it seemed liked Déjà vu. Years after she had given her heart to God as a child, she was now sitting in the same church, on what seemed to be a random Sunday, on a random trip back home. She began to weep uncontrollably. She sat remembering how God had spoken to her heart as a little girl. Time seemed to stand still for her. There, she sat in the small country church having an unplanned encounter with God.

She remembered being just twelve years old. Her life goal then was to become a missionary. Her heart's desire was to rescue young girls who were being abused. God had planted a seed in her years ago and oddly, now, it was emerging from the soil.

What would she do now? She sat there torn between her will and God's will.

She returned to the city and sat down with the president of the company. He was blown away at what he heard. She was willing to give up the job if they would not allow her to fulfill her calling to the mission field. Tammy was respectable, honorable, and people had great faith in her. She had a golden reputation. The president looked across the table and said, "I don't see why we can't allow the call upon your life to mesh with the career of a lifetime." She stood up and shook his hand.

Every year, Tammy raises her own funds to cross the ocean as a missionary rescuing an untold number of young girls from human sex trafficking. She was willing to walk away from millions to fulfill God's blueprint for her life if the company rejected her offer. She found the blueprint and followed it. That is what real, raw faith is about.

We all truly have a destiny. It may not be to become a missionary and sleep on the jungle floors but then again it may be! Your divine blueprint may be to manage a fortune 500 company, or it may be to be a farmer who feeds the community and the world.

God calls us all into different fields of life. None of us are exactly the same. We may share some passions, but we are uniquely different as well. I joke with people that pastoring is what I do for my living, but preaching is what I do for my loving. God places us all in fields of occupation and those occupations are platforms for God to work.

NO TWO ALIKE

Royce McClure is the designer of one of the world's largest jigsaw puzzles. The puzzle is called "LIFE: The Great Challenge." The puzzle contains 24,000 pieces that all fit perfectly together. When he was asked about the greatest challenge behind designing this puzzle, Royce responded, "The challenge for me in a puzzle of this size was to eliminate large areas where no changes take place," (Way, 2010, p. 3). In other words, he did not want any two pieces to be dull or boring while sitting beside each other in the puzzle. The entire puzzle needs the individual pieces, but the detail of those pieces won't be clearly seen until they are all put together.

Now think about the God of the Bible who has marvelously formed all things according to His own purpose and plan. He, as the grand designer, has formed everything under the sun for a specific time, season, and purpose! You are included in this plan! God placed you in this life. He placed you here as a piece of His puzzle and plan. You are either running toward God and embracing His call on your life, or you are running away from God and doing life on your own terms.

The concept of a giant puzzle in the hands of a great designer is the ultimate metaphor for the relationship between Creator God and us. We are God's workmanship. We are His big redemptive canvas. We are not all the same shape, size, or color. Yet, we fit somewhere in God's puzzle.

So, let me ask you a question: do you feel like you are trying to cram a piece of the puzzle into a space that simply doesn't fit? Oh my! God doesn't create confused people. You may be trying to fit God into *your* life or theology. Self-identifying yourself and then acting as though it is a holy thing is evil. Stop trying to cram God into your life. Surrender and give your life to the Lord Jesus Christ. Then, what will happen is the Master Potter will take you like clay and shape, mold, and place you into His plan. This was His intent all along. Whenever you submit to God, your occupational or spiritual calling may not come with spa treatment and soft padding to make you more than comfortable, but you will have an inner knowing from the Holy Spirit that this is right where you are meant to be. Get in the plan and let the plan get inside of you. Don't run from what seems to be hard. God will empower you to do what He has called you to do. The world is waiting!

THE BOLDPRINT

> **MANY PIECES, ONE PUZZLE.**
> **WE *ALL* FIT IN GOD'S PUZZLE!**

CHAPTER FIVE
DUCT TAPE, MONEY, & CLOCKS

In the book of Ecclesiastes one of the main themes is eternity.

"He has made everything beautiful in its time. He has also *set eternity in the human heart*, yet[a] no one can fathom what God has done from beginning to end." **Ecclesiastes 3:11, New International Version**

God doesn't live in time, we do. Everything we do is revolving around a clock. For most people, time is the measuring stick of their day-to-day life. We go into work at a certain time. We get kids from school at a certain time. We try to get into bed around a certain time. Time is ticking all around us. There is a clock in your hands right now. It's called a phone.

We have alarms set for everything. Due to the fact that we are victims of this fast-paced culture we have become guilty of becoming extremely impatient. This way of life has trained us that we can have most things at the touch of a button.

The Bible is full of the three-fold cord of faith, patience, and process. Countless scriptures tell us what real faith is. Countless scriptures teach us that with great patience, we reap a harvest. Countless scriptures reveal to us that without process, we can't be molded by grace into the image of Christ. Resistance is a part of life. I'd say a huge part. Resistance can be anything that brings exhaustion or stress to you. God uses pressure, resistance, and disappointments to shape and mold us. If you meet someone who has never had any level of resistance in life, you have probably met a narcissist.

Kids who are raised without love suffer from feelings of abandonment. Kids who are raised without being taught responsibility and perseverance become weak-willed adults who can't process real life. What farmer doesn't need to have faith to believe as he is planting a small seed that it will become a large harvest? What farmer is discouraged if he doesn't see a harvest only one day after planting seeds? Process requires time and season. Having to wait on God and going through trials will develop patience in you… If you let it!

THREE FAITH TRAPS TO AVOID

There are three things that often prevent us from reaching out in faith to seize the plan of God for our lives:

1. A Duct Tape Mentality

This mentality is not biblical. God never tells us to settle down into a mindset of *good enough*. *Good enough* believes that where you are currently in your walk with Christ is simply good enough. Growth is always a part of our walk with God and we are never beyond needing grace to press on. This mentality is against reaching for anything that is better than good in this life. We even have teachers and ministries that teach this bad bread. There are people who actually believe that the poorer you are, the more spiritual you must be. While the Bible tells us that godliness with contentment is great gain and the love of money is the root of all evil, it also tells us countless times that God is our Provider and the One who is pleased to prosper us. Having possessions and owning things is not a sin.

The devil will whisper "You'll never have anything. You'll never rise to the top. You'll never make any more money than this." All of this is to get you into a duct tape mentality. You will begin to take ownership of these lies and even feed the idea that this is a permanent reality. Next, you will get into a negative pattern of thinking and begin to speak death over your situation. Often times, when resistance comes, we get into a pattern of thinking "If it were not for bad luck, I would have no luck at all." Don't fall into this trap.

Don't try to duct tape things in your life that God has called you to disregard, destroy, or put away. The first step to claiming any *promised land* promises that God has given you is to walk in the direction of that promised land even while you are standing in the middle of the parched desert. That is faith at its finest! Throw the duct tape away. Believe God for the best and let Him shape you in the worst.

2. A Lack of Money

I would say that the majority of the time that there is a money issue inside of a home, it usually boils down to money management, rather than a lack of money.

Nevertheless, along with the duct tape mentality of "just getting by," the enemy will send into your pathway the "money trial." This usually holds us back in our faith and it has nothing to do with money. There hasn't been one-time God hasn't supplied the need for my family, but I can tell you there has been a ton of close calls. God allows the brooks to dry up in our lives for a variety of reasons, but never to watch us suffer or complain. Don't view the will of God through the lens cap of your bank account. God is not moved, swayed, or threatened by a lack of money or too much money. God put gold on the streets of Heaven, so He isn't moved by our monetary mountains. Trust Him. Don't fall into the devil's trap of a lack of supply. He will only show you your present struggle. He will only show pieces of the truth. God will supply the need. Your job is to be willing and obedient.

3. Time

They say that time is a cruel mistress. Well, that may be true or may not be, but either way she has a clock on her belt! She tends to whip us with it every day. We live and we die by the clock in our hand. This *time trap* is a classic tactic from the enemy.

What happens is we don't see God's will coming to pass in our time frame. The promises haven't come to pass in a manner we so desired and now we are somewhat discouraged. Have we become slaves to the technology in our hands? I think so. We want it and we want it now. God doesn't work that way.

There are three responses from God to our prayers: yes, no, and wait. All three answers are biblical and bring out the best possible solution for the child of God.

Man is born with the concept of eternity ingrained inside of his DNA. To believe that we just live and then we die is simply non-sense. Most people I know, even those who are unbelievers or participate in other religions, believe that there is a life after this present one. Every human conscience screams out that there is something more than this present life. The reality of eternity has been planted in the heart of man, even if we cannot fully conceive it. God has placed within you the ability to understand that there is a finish line somewhere in your future. Don't fall into the trap of "it hasn't happened yet." Submit to God's calendar. Trust me, it's worth the wait.

PRINCIPLES. PROMISES. PATTERNS.

When God draws, he uses an indelible pen. God has written *principles* for us to live by. They bring blessings into our life. God has written *promises* for His children. These promises are often discovered through fiery trials and great patience! Lastly, God draws *patterns* on the tablet of our heart. Many times, the current frustration that we are feeling, if excavated, is really our inner man seeking out what God has already written upon our heart. In other words, the very blueprint that God has written upon the tablet of our heart will not sit silent. That call will absolutely haunt us until we are drawn unto its author. This is where life really begins.

We are born in this world *head* first, but we are born into the next world (God's Kingdom), *heart* first. In your heart, God has designed a divine blueprint that can only be fully understood by you finding the will of God. You simply meandering through this life is not God's will. A great life isn't born from the ground of a shallow heart. A great soul is not formed by lucky moments or good fortune, but rather by being in submission to the will of God for your WHOLE life. The will of God for you is just that personal!

SHOW ME THE MONEY

The chief priests and teachers of the law came to Jesus. Their goal was to trap Him into breaking the law to have Him arrested. They listened intently and watched Him like a hawk. They sent spies to probe Him with questions. In Luke 20, one of the questions was concerning paying taxes.

"Is it lawful for us to give tribute unto Caesar, or no? But he perceived their craftiness, and said unto them, Why tempt ye me? Shew me a penny. Whose image and superscription hath it? They answered and said, Caesar's. And he said unto them, Render therefore unto Caesar the things which be Caesar's, and unto God the things which be God's. And they could not take hold of his words before the people: and they marvelled at his answer, and held their peace." **Luke 20:22-26, King James Version**

The question was a trap, but the answer was packed with deliverance. Jesus asked them for a penny. A symbol of exchange in their culture. On that coin was the image of Caesar. Jesus had them trapped now. Whose image was on the coin? Caesar's. So, what was that question leading to?

Jesus was answering their question with a question. The real question was whose image was upon them? The question wasn't *what* their life looked like but rather *who* it looked like. The coin belonged to Caesar and it was his property. Whose image were they and who had the rights to their life? Jesus had them right where He wanted them! They were stumped and held their peace.

God has created you in His image but also placed His image upon you. God placed His markings upon you. Just as my son is my son through the simple fact that his mother gave birth to him. Yet, his image is very similar to that of his dad. My wife calls him my twin. I'm his father biologically, but you wouldn't need a blood test to believe that. The resemblance is overwhelming.

The real *you* will not be found until you are born again. God isn't lost. He's been looking for you. The moment you put your faith in the Lordship of Jesus, He removes the scales of years of blindness and you can finally see the real you. You'll find yourself in Him. If you try to find contentment and fulfillment anywhere else, you'll be disappointed.

DON'T BE STUPID

Eternity has been placed in our hearts. Something deep inside of us tells us that we are going to live forever somewhere. The human conscience yells out the great truth that eternity is real. The reality of eternity has been planted in our hearts by God, Himself. The concept of time seems so elusive. The days seem to be so long, but the years seem so short.

Have you ever heard anyone make the statement "I'm taking it one day at a time?" Guess who else is? Everyone! That's how time works! You can't take it one month at a time or one year at a time. Many writers in the New Testament laid great emphasis on the subject of *the brevity of life*. Look at what Paul and James both wrote:

"Be very careful, then, how you live—not as unwise but as wise, making the most of every opportunity, because the days are evil.

"Therefore, do not be foolish, but understand what the Lord's will is." **Ephesians 5:15-17, New International Version**

"Why, you do not even know what will happen tomorrow. What is your life? You are a mist that appears for a little while and then vanishes." **James 4:14, New International Version**

The Bible beats on the door of our heart. It shouts out "Be wise! Get wisdom! Use wisdom!"

My favorite translation of Ephesians 5:15-17, is found in the Contemporary Version. It reads **"Act like people with good sense and not like fools. These are evil times, so make every minute count. Don't be stupid. Instead, find out what the Lord wants you to do."**

This translation is astounding. The Bible literally commands us to not be stupid in relation to the will of God. Profound indeed!

Life comes at you fast. The blueprint for your life is not disconnected from the body of Christ. Being saved and not attending church is like being married and never going home. Your destiny is not just about you! God's plan is not meant to be a part of your life. Your life is meant to be a part of God's plan. Your piece of the puzzle can't be disconnected from the entire puzzle itself. Together these pieces form the beautiful canvas of God in this earth. That canvas is called the glorious Body of Christ. Your blueprint affects others. It's that simple!

We don't know how long we have here on this earth. Death calls both the young and old. The finish line for our earthly lives is hidden from us all. None of us have any clue when we will cross the finish line of life and step into eternity. God has a plan for you. As basic as that sounds, it is very biblical. The Bible is full of people who seem to be super-human, fairy tale characters, or from another universe. On the contrast, they were flesh and blood just as you are. These people found their blueprint, whether it came through unusual circumstance, trial, or God's providence. How important do you think it was for Joseph to walk into his blueprint? Joseph fulfilling the will of God for his life literally saved his family and their nation from starvation.

I hear people talk about their family situations and I always want to ask them "Have you been sold as a slave by your family?" Joseph was! His trial literally saved the entire nation of Israel. God's first plan for you is to save you. God, then, places you in His kingdom and unveils His plan for your *earthly pilgrimage*.

OCCUPY TIL I COME

"And he called his ten servants, and delivered them ten pounds, and said unto them, Occupy till I come." **Luke 19:13, King James Version**

One time I read the phrase "occupy till I come" and my spirit erupted with insight. God doesn't save us to simply stick us in a church. Our role is not to simply *occupy* a church until God does something else bigger. There are two commands in this verse:

1. *Occupy.* 2. *Until I Come.*

What does this mean? Well, it means-engage, do business, trade, invest. This verse uses money as an example of what the heirs of the kingdom are to do. We are to be spent! We as Christians are not to sit in the corner silent while society falls apart. We are to speak up and let our voice be heard. God didn't save us and drown us in a baptismal tank, nor plant us in a safe greenhouse, but rather He planted us high on the mountain. We are positioned where the sun beats down the hottest and the rain falls the hardest. The church has a right to its voice.

Jesus Christ was aware of the society that He lived in. He commanded people to pay their taxes. Paul tells us to pray for leaders (good or bad). He writes in the book of Romans about military personnel and police. They don't bear the sword in vain. There is no separation in the Old or New Testament with the involvement of God's people in what's going on in the world. We are to occupy. Let me explain:

We are not to sit on a hill and forget the city or sit around contemplating or criticizing everything. Everyone doesn't need to be employed by a church in the Christian world. We need people in the world of business, government, politics and the practical vocations of life. That's where the lost are! John the Baptist believed that he could occupy and have a voice in his generation. He confronted the sin of his society. Jesus interacted with and ministered to Roman politicians of His day. He even healed a centurion's servant.

We are to occupy until Jesus comes. What do you do for a living? It's not nearly as important as asking yourself *"Am I doing what God placed me on this earth to do?"* I look around and I see people making a living and losing their life. In our society, we aim to be successful and very often we reach that goal but end up losing our soul. Money and greed have pinned us into the corner of deception and bondage. We believe that through pursuing materialistic things that we are being set free, but in reality, we are being put into bondage. As stated earlier, God is not against things. It's when these things become our deepest affection and desire that we fall into the sin of idolatry.

"Occupy until I come" is Jesus' way of telling us that we are to get into the field called life! America is consumed with a protest mentality. It seems like we are protesting everything. I believe the greatest war that we are fighting is a spiritual war. I do believe we should do all that is within our power to stand and fight for what is right; from those who write the laws of the land, right down to the ones who go to the polls to vote. I honestly believe that it's all a part of the enemy's plan to cause such a ruckus over everyone protesting everything under the sun, that we as believers are tempted to just "shut our mouth and give up." Yet, we cannot do this!

So, what are we to do?

Well, we need to shine the light of Christ more than we shout about *what* we believe. That is not to say we should not preach what we believe...but we should practice what we believe first. We are to live a life full of grace and truth. We don't have to forsake either of these principles!

We must *stand* for the rights of the unborn.
We must *stand* for the children of this land and others.
We must *stand* for Biblical marriage.
We must love God and our neighbor as ourselves.
However, we must NOT *stand* in a position of pride, but rather love.

Jesus never once mocked or made fun of anyone that we see in the Bible. Still, He never ventured away from what was true. If you are reading this, I have no condemnation for you. True freedom is rooted in the truth and nothing less. It is the truth that sets you free. Truth knows no political party. We are to occupy until He comes. Whatever field God has called you to, you need to shine for Christ. I'm not talking about going to work and causing disorder over what you believe. I'm talking about simply being there for people and being salt and light until He comes.

"DON'T BE STUPID." IT'S A COMMAND.

CHAPTER SIX

THE FIGHT, MY COURSE, & THE FAITH

"I have fought a good fight, I have finished my course, and I have kept the faith."
2 Timothy 4:7, King James Version

THE GOOD FIGHT

Sometimes we feel like we don't have any fight left in our fight. Life can take us to the highest of highs and drop us to the lowest of lows. We are never as strong as we think we are, and we aren't as weak as our flesh tries to convince us we are. The older I get, the more I realize how strong God was in me at different times in my life. The devil will do his best to identify us by our greatest weaknesses. This isn't a new tactic. God defines us by one victory and it's not a victory we won. God defines us by the victory that His Son, Jesus, won for us on the cross.

The fight is already fixed and decided. God has destined us to win. Let's agree that every rational human born of the womb will have a variety of battles in this life. This life is good, but it also brings the results of the curse of sin: tears, sorrow, and heartache. Everyone has a fight to win or lose. I hear people say, "It's hard to be rich," then I want to say, "It's hard to be poor." Which hard do you want? You never lose in God until you are unwilling to fight. You are not fighting alone. God has taped your hands with grace and mercy. The gloves to this fight are taped securely around your wrist. You aren't going to win every round of this fight. You're going to win some rounds and you're going to lose some rounds. The key to victory is to know that God has set up this fight with your victory in mind. God uses our defeats to build us up. Often times, the fights that we have to contend with are intended to break us and allow the oil of humility to get inside of our wounded soul. We don't see the sneaky pride, subtle disobedience, and hidden agendas that creep into our daily life.

The bottom line is that we become very self-sufficient. This is a recipe for delayed victory. God desires our total dependence upon Him in, during, and after the fight. Giving up isn't surrendering. Surrendering to God is releasing Him and the invisible allies of Heaven to fight your battles for you. People often make statements of doubt like "Well, I'm just going to give up. What's the use in trying?" Giving up is a lack of faith in God. God never calls us to throw in the towel. Rather than throwing in the towel, God wants us to begin to wave the towel of victory. Never are we more alive than when we are serving, helping, and encouraging others! Jesus took a towel and served. God never calls us to give up, rather He calls us to surrender to Him. Surrender is our part; the victory is God's part. In the end we should be able to say that the fight was *good*.

DESTINED FOR IT

You were born, and you will die. It's what happens in between these two that matters the most. God doesn't save us to simply stick us inside of a church until He comes. The first plan God has for His people is to redeem them through His Son, Jesus. The second plan is to deploy them into His plan for their life. The word *destiny* seems to be very popular in modern Christianity. It has become the theme of much of what we see on a bookshelf all around. Paul wrote to the church at Thessalonica these words, "…so that no one would be unsettled by these trials. For you know quite well that we are destined for them." **I Thessalonians 3:3, New International Version**

These Christians in Thessalonica were under severe persecutions and Paul had the audacity to tell them that this was a part of their destiny. It sounds strange to be called by God to endure adversity, resistance, and trials that seem to overwhelm us. You can rest assured that our blueprint will come with road blocks, delays, and detours. Our destiny includes headaches, heartaches, losses, and crosses along the way. Don't forget that we know

Christ in His death and suffering, but we also know Him in His resurrection and victory. Our destiny also comes with the peace, joy, and happiness of knowing Him and His blessings. The full gospel that Jesus preached embraces both sides of our destiny and every page of our blueprint-the good and bad. Living for God comes with the blessing of God, and the same faith that you sense when you are on top of the mountain will be the same faith you will need when you experience great offense.

MY COURSE

The course God has given us to run is solely designed for us. The strength of this three-fold cord here is what the Apostle Paul called "my (it belonged to him) course." We may never run our course but, nevertheless it belongs to us. He understood that his entire life was drawn up like the lane of a running track. He understood that just as a runner has been assigned a lane, we, as well, have been given a blueprint that will bring God glory IF we stay in our lane!

This idea of *running our course* is not a new one. It is mentioned at least two times in the book of Acts in reference to David and John the Baptist. David is said to have "served his own generation by the will of God." John the Baptist is said to have "fulfilled his course". Paul states in Acts 20:24 (King James Version) "…so that I might finish my course with joy." The majority of people who are born never realize that there was a blueprint for their life. They simply are alive. They never truly live. They never know, or they know but never get into **their** *lane* to run **their** *course.*

The saddest thing to see is a life without shadows. A life that never left a mark is a sad one indeed. A shadowless life is a life that knew its worth but went without application. How many of our present problems are connected to the simple fact that we got off the course that God designed for us to run in and ran in another direction? Sadly, when we do this, we end up running in circles.

WHO ARE YOU RACING?

We are trained by our culture to slow down long enough to look around at all the other runners in the race and see what they are doing. We are trained to compete with what others are doing in this life. The Bible teaches us to run with the Spirit of God and not to compare our lives with others.

"Since we live by the Spirit, let us keep in step with the Spirit."
Galatians 5:25, New International Version

I love this verse. Staying in stride with the Holy Spirit is as vital as anything else you can find in the New Testament. We tend to race *against* the Spirit instead of racing *with* the Spirit. By doing this, we forfeit His strength. Run your race, empowered with the voice of the Holy Spirit within. We are instructed as we run to not run or labor in vain. We are not to simply run or fight in this life at random.

How can you run your course?

7. Spiritually eat and drink RIGHT.
6. Train for your race.
5. Lay aside all sins or weights that easily hold you back.
4. Stay in your lane.
3. Don't stare at others in different lanes.
2. Stay focused.
1. Don't look back.

Are you trying to outrun your past? Stop. In Christ, your past has been forgiven.

Are you trying to outrun what you see on social media from others? Stop. Competing with others is not God's plan for YOU.

Are you trying to outrun God? ***Impossible.***

When we run in God, then we run with God's strength and grace. When we run in our own plans, purposes, and power, then we run in what strength *we* have, and the result is that we end up running in circles. Running in God means that we run through time into eternity with victory. I don't want to leave this world wrong, but rather STRONG!

THE FAITH

It's not about how righteous we are. It's about us believing that

God has made us righteous through His Son's atoning sacrifice. God not only saves us, but He is able to keep us. Paul kept the faith, but in reality, the faith kept him. What good would the fight have been if Paul had gotten to the end of his life and died in doubt or unbelief? A part of our faith in Jesus Christ is not only what I call *saving faith* but also *keeping faith*. Not one of us use a different type of grace than the next person. It's God's grace. Someone may say "Well, grace isn't cheap." My response is simply "Yes, I know…it's free." If it's not free, we can't afford it. I can assure you of that.

Often times, we have faith to believe God loves us enough to get us out of our sin pit, but rarely do we have the faith to believe He loves us if we jump back into that pit. We don't pretend to act like God is in agreement with our sin, in fact, He hates it, but He hates the effects it has on His child far more.

The child of God is not the one who sins less than the next person, but rather the one whose sins are covered by the blood of Jesus. Our faith in Christ is not only a believing faith, but also a faith that keeps us. Somewhere in our journey with God, we tend to lose ground. We don't necessarily lose our salvation, but often times the joy evaporates and peace seems hard to find.

If the blueprint that God has drawn for us is the very tailor-made course we are to run in this life, then our faith in God is the very strength to finish the race strong. Our focus is Jesus Christ. He is the prize of the high-calling. If we keep the faith, it will keep us!

THE BOLDPRINT

DON'T THROW IN THE TOWEL, WAVE IT IN VICTORY!

CHAPTER SEVEN

BUILD IT GOD'S WAY

THE GOD VIEW

God sees the end from the beginning. God is standing at every curve watching every moment of our lives. There is nothing hidden from the all-seeing eye of God. God declared the end from the beginning and has set in motion the element of time and all of its components under His sovereignty. The eyes of God see what none other can see, from the vast earth to the very hairs on our head. God knows the beginning, sees the present, and is already standing in the future. Jesus not only sees the beginning of all things, but also the end. He himself said "I am Alpha and Omega, the beginning and the ending, saith the Lord, which is, and which was, and which is to come, the Almighty." **Revelation 1:8, King James Version**

Jesus Christ is the first song of all of Heaven and He will be the centerpiece of the last song!

THE REGRET BOOTH

When this life is over, will you have to stop by the regret booth and sit for a while? Will you be full of regret at the end of this life? The regret booth is like the dunk tank at a cheap carnival. It has a long line of people ready to throw the ball at the victim. The only problem is that the dunk tank is full of bacteria. The more regret we allow to eat us, the more poison sets up inside of us. Now, there are some things in life we are going to regret. It's close to impossible to have no regrets. This is simply a byproduct of being human. Yet, many live in a state of mind of constant regret. This is wasteful living. Often, I think of things I wish I could have done differently. Yet, what good is regret? We can't go back to yesterday. We can only use it to teach us what not to do.

THE OFFENSE BANK

When this life is over, will you be sitting at the offense bank? This is the place where all the offenses that you have allowed to take your joy will be stored up with no profitable interest. Offense breeds debate. When there is a lack of forgiveness over what was done to us or said about us, we are allowing the opportunity for offense to take root. The only fruit of offense is bitterness. The only fruit of bitterness is hate. The only fruit of hate is a strong delusion. The individual who has allowed the full harvest of offense to come has now given themselves over to a particular blindness that is very difficult to shake off. Usually the person is unaware of this blindness. Offense simply breeds debate. All we want to do when we are offended is to argue our points with the other party. It's similar to being on the high school debate team, but you never win. We are too busy thinking of points to prove others wrong rather than focusing on real solutions. Yet, if we give our bitterness to the Lord, He will in turn use those hurts as the foundation that He builds our lives upon. You will have more than a past of offense, you'll have a future full of testimony.

There are people all around us that are not living life according to their divine blueprint, simply because of regret and offense.

RUNNING BACKWARDS IS BEST

In this life, we face situations that have no real answers on this side of Heaven. Often, we must trust in God without answers. God doesn't give explanations. God gives commands! These commands bring blessings into our life if they are heeded and obeyed. Eternity will reveal what time did conceal. God's point of view is comprehensive. He sees it all! Once a person sees the blueprints for their life, it's time to run backwards. I know it sounds crazy. No, God doesn't want us living in the past. No, God doesn't want us looking over our shoulders at what is behind us. What I am talking about is being obedient to the blueprint God showed you at different moments of your life.

Well, when I was a boy, I had a vision one night and, in the vision, I saw myself preaching. In this vision I was a thirty-something-year-old man. My first thought was "God, I can't do that."

Yet, just as God showed Moses the Promised Land from high atop the mountain, God will show you a glimpse of where He is taking you. God drops hints and clues. These are sent to build your faith in Him. God will often tell us who, what, when, or where but rarely will He tell us HOW! This is how our faith matures into something that isn't shaken by the winds of rejection, adversity, or fear. Once you see the vision God has for you, then off you go! Run toward the goal. You may have to release people who have offended you or hurt you. Misery will come to the one who fails to see the blueprint God has for them. What a miserable life to know God had a tailor-made plan for you, but you lived in the state of *self* or simply resisted His blueprint for your life. In my dream, I saw myself as a grown man preaching. So, what did I do? I began to run in that direction.

I saw the future before it arrived. Then, in faith, I began to run backwards and catch up with the little boy who had that vision. He is a grown man now.

PATTERN FROM THE MOUNTAIN

God called Israel His firstborn Son. When Israel came out of slavery from the Egyptians, God had promised them a land all their own. God called this land a "promised' land. Israel would have to walk through a wilderness before they would ever see this promised land. Their lives were surrounded by a structure called *the church in the wilderness*. This church was a tabernacle that served as a portable place of worship that required set up and tear down as they traveled throughout the wilderness for the purpose of worship unto God.

The worship of the people was a serious matter in the eyes of God. At any time of the day, the trumpet would blow, and they would have to pack up the entire church and march forward. Can you imagine how difficult this must have been? How did this tabernacle originally come about?

"And let them make me a sanctuary; that I may dwell among them. According to all that I shew thee, after the pattern of the tabernacle, and the pattern of all the instruments thereof, even so shall ye make it." **Exodus 25:8-9, King James Version**

God brought Moses to the top of the mountain and gave him a pattern. God told Moses to make sure that he or the people did not waver one bit on this tabernacle design. God gave an entire nation a blueprint that they were to build their lives around. Yet, there was one condition and it was simple-Israel must build this tabernacle EXACTLY according to God's blueprint.

"Study the design you were given on the mountain and make everything accordingly." **Exodus 25:40, The Message Translation**

This tabernacle would house the God of Heaven. His glory would appear inside of this tabernacle. This *church in the wilderness* was the centerpiece of their nation's entire existence. Literally, the twelve tribes lived surrounding this tabernacle. Now, for the record, they didn't live ten feet from the front door, but off in the distance they could see the tabernacle. This served as a daily reminder that the centerpiece of their life was worship and that worship belonged to God Almighty.

HOUSE PLANS

Now, the Bible teaches us that this Old Testament glory was to be done away with. God revealed Himself to a nation and when Christ came, God revealed Himself to the world! In the New Testament, we are God's tabernacle. We are His temple! In the same way God gave Moses this pattern or blueprint for him and the nation, is the same way God gives it to us believers today! We are now the temples of the Holy Spirit. We are the body of Christ! Every person that has come to know Christ must surrender to His saving grace **and** Lordship. Once you have come to know Christ, He begins to show you His blueprint for your life! Salvation in Christ plus nothing gets you to Heaven. However, if you are going to do the will of God in this earth, you must seek the Lord concerning what His blueprint is for your life.

BLUEPRINTS GONE BAD

The Bible is full of people who found the blueprint for their life, such as Joseph. Think about what Joseph had to endure to truly walk into the very purpose and blueprint that God had drawn up for him. He fully recognized that God was the grand Seamster pulling all the strings of his life together for the good. Joseph himself said these words:

"You plotted evil against me, but God turned it into good, in order to preserve the lives of many people who are alive today because of what happened." **Genesis 50:20, Good News Translation**

The Bible is also full of people who not only missed the marks on their blueprint, but missed the entire target altogether.

Think about King Saul who was chosen by the people and anointed by God to lead a nation, but never really lived up to his full potential. Saul, through mere disobedience, ultimately died in shame.

Think about Absalom, who was the son of King David. In all Israel there was none quite like him. From the soles of his feet to the crown of his head, there wasn't a blemish on him. He was known for his long hair. In the ancient times, long hair was considered a landmark of a warrior's prowess and strength. Yet, through his lies, deception, and rebellion he died completely outside of the will of God. His long hair became his short fall. Absalom was riding a mule under a great oak tree and the unthinkable happened. His head was caught up between branches and he hung there and died. What blueprint God must have had for Saul, the first king and Absalom, David's son. Those blueprints were never fulfilled.

How important is it to you to have God's blueprint for your life? We don't go to college without a plan. We don't get married without a plan and purpose. We spend years thinking about who Mr. or Mrs. Right will be. We want to spend the rest of our lives with this person so a little homework on this subject is a great idea. Most of us don't even to go on vacation without a game plan. What value can be placed on our education, marrying the right person, or purchasing the right home? These are all life-changing decisions that biblically beckon us to look up for direction. If God can show Moses a blueprint for an entire nation, then God can show you His blueprint for you as an individual.

THE BOLDPRINT

> ### SEE THE FUTURE AND
> ### RUN BACKWARDS!

CHAPTER EIGHT

BURNING BUSHES

Déjà vu is the feeling that you have already experienced something that is actually happening for the first time.

Moses killed a man in Egypt in defense of his Hebrew brothers. After this, he fled in fear for his life. He fled to the land of Midian. Here, he went to work for his future father-in-law, Jethro, as a shepherd. It was in this season of life that something incredible happened. He comes to what the Bible calls "the backside of the desert." Here, something supernatural is about to unfold.

The angel of the Lord appears to him in a flame of fire out of a bush. Moses is perplexed and bewildered at the sight of this bush blazing with fire. The bush was burning, but not being consumed. Only God can do this. The world will set you on fire with fake love, success, or fame and in the end, you will be burnt like toast! God will fill you up and your life will overflow with the fire of good things, leaving no bad after taste.

Moses draws near to the bush and a voice comes from the bush. God tells Moses to take off his shoes. This is a sacred moment. This is a holy moment. This is a moment that Moses will never forget.

"And he (God) said, Certainly I will be with thee; and this shall be a *token* unto thee, that I have sent thee: When thou hast brought forth the people out of Egypt, ye shall serve God upon this mountain." **Exodus 3:12, King James Version**

GOD TOKENS

God gives tokens. Tokens are hints, clues, and signs. Tokens are representing reminders of what God has done or something God is going to do. Of course, we don't sit around day in and day out allowing all of our energies to be consumed by looking for a sign from Heaven. On the contrary, we walk by faith and God gives us tokens of His presence and direction as we grow and move in faith. Direction matters to God. It's only when we begin to move in His direction that He usually drops our marching orders in front of us. God will order our steps if we will take them!

Moses needed a token. This burning bush was just that- a token from God.

Moses seems, to me, like a man not necessarily running from God but not really running toward God either. He is just in a season where he is a simple shepherd. In Exodus 3, Moses is now a family man. He is married and he has children. Here is where it would be very easy to just drift further out into the sea of shadowless living. God gives him this bush as the ultimate token of providence. Moses is about to find out that he will come back to this very spot.

Everyone needs a burning bush.

Moses only got one bush his entire life, so we should live in such a way that we are aware of God's providential tokens. These moments are invaluable and may only come around once in a lifetime. Wake up!

God gives tokens. I personally believe God gives us tokens of direction as we move toward His will in full faith. Did you hear what the scripture said? The Lord told him that he would return to this mountain, but this time he would be leading an entire nation. Wow! The burning bush would become déjà vu for Moses. He would return to Egypt to deliver God's people and then he would return to this very mountain. God gave him the token that he would come full circle. In due time, he would be back.

I can't count the times that I have walked into situations where I felt like I had been there before. I used to have dreams of different encounters that would come to pass in days or years ahead. I have circled mountains that I knew I would have to climb or pass again at some point. When God gives you a burning bush through circumstances, blessings, or trials, stop long enough to take your shoes off and worship God. You'll need that strength when you come to the next giant you face.

I can only imagine what Moses was thinking after the Exodus miracle was over and the people were approaching Mt. Horeb. He had been here before! Déjà vu!! This time, he would receive the very law of God and the pattern to the tabernacle during this visit. He had come full circle indeed.

THE PERFECT SENTENCE

A college professor was teaching one day in class and asked her students to compose the perfect sentence. The class spent many sessions brainstorming about the assignment. Such subjects as family, God, sex, and fame were numerous. Adjectives like passionate, full, essential, empty, and awesome all came up.

The professor then told the class the perfect sentence was found in the Bible. She told them that in Exodus 3, God gave us the perfect sentence. She told them the story of Moses standing with bare feet in front of this blazing bush. In Exodus 3 Moses and the Lord have a back and forth conversation about how this exodus will happen. Moses is confounded by this exodus feat that lies ahead of him. Moses says to God, "Who am I?" You can hear the insecurity and fear in his voice.

"And Moses said unto God, Behold, when I come unto the children of Israel, and shall say unto them, The God of your fathers hath sent me unto you; and they shall say to me, What is his name? What shall I say unto them? And God said unto Moses, I AM THAT I AM: and he said, Thus shalt thou say unto the children of Israel, I AM hath sent me unto you."
Exodus 3:14, King James Version

The professor then explained that the perfect sentence was "I am that I am."

If this sentence could be translated it would mean:

"He, in distinction from all others, is the only true God, the God who really is the eternal, self-existent, immutable being. The only being who can say that He always will be what He always has been." (Cetas, 2009, p.4)

I AM WHO I AM. The name tells us who God is. He is the God in the present moment, in our darkest past, and in all of our tomorrows. The God of the Bible is a God of all seasons. There is not a season of your life that God has not been present. Perhaps you have pushed God away and you feel distant and disconnected from Him. There's never been a moment that the Holy Spirit did not desire a relationship with you. You can

94

spiritually come home today.

LOOK BOTH WAYS BEFORE CROSSING

Remember when you crossed the street as a kid and the adult with you said, "Always look both ways before you cross the street?" This is true of life itself. The wise man considers well where he is, where he has been, and where he is going. Whether we want it to or not, life teaches us to look both ways. Perspective sometimes comes to us high on the mountain of victory. But more often, perspective comes to us through dark trials or circumstances. It is in the night seasons of our life that we tend to stop long enough to gain God's perspective.

Mountains and valleys are a part of this life. There are three types of mountains:

*Mt. Perspective

*Mt. Retrospective

*Mt. Comprehensive

A mountain of perspective is when we are aware enough to stand and see the land ahead of us that is still unclaimed. God usually has come into our lives to slow us down long enough to get our attention. A cat won't sit on a hot stove. But, if he ever has, he will never sit on a cold one either! God uses every day, ordinary things to give us perspective. Through a variety of circumstances, I personally have gained valuable perspective. Whether it was disappointment with people or even failures in my own life, I have learned a lot from a dummy-even if at times that dummy was me! I love the perspective I get from others. It's free. You can learn from others' mistakes and you can learn from your own.

A mountain of retrospection is when we stand in a season of our life and allow God to put the lantern on the back part of the ship. The wise man considers well where he is going. The best way he does this is by not forgetting where he has been. This mountain of retrospection is where we stand high atop the mountain and gaze at the land that has already been claimed. Look at how far you have come! For most of us, the past has its dark places of regret but at the same time it also holds such a wealth of wisdom. Have you stared long enough at what is behind you to learn the lessons that the past has given you? There is a storehouse in your chemistry for the things that have happened in your life. It's called memory. Memory is a powerful thing. In order for something to be a real memory, it has to earn its way into your memory bank. Past wounds have to go deep enough to become a scar. This scar is a memorial or token that you will testify about in due time. Nothing is wasted if God is in the situation. Defeat has no power where real grace is present. Every loss is a win in God's grace. How is that possible? It's only a true loss if we haven't gained the lessons, blessings, and wisdom that God desires to bring to us through our failures. Something must leave an impression to really be remembered. Don't miss this mountain.

A comprehensive mountain is my favorite. Often when life has beat us up enough, God will put us on a mountain where we can clearly see all sides of our situation: the past, the present, and the future! Moses got this comprehensive view at the burning bush. He could stare toward Egypt and remember. He also could have camped out barefooted at the fiery bush and just kept God's miraculous power to himself. Yet, he could also see where God was taking him and the nation. Occasionally, God will place me atop this mountain where He will show me where He has brought me from, make me aware of where I currently am, and show me pieces of His plan for the future. This is the place where God says, "Look both ways before crossing."

Do you know what you are doing right now?

You are making memories, so make them good. On one hand you have to have lived long enough to "look both ways" but on the other hand, gray hair won't necessarily make you wise either. You can be a young fool, or you can be an old fool. Wisdom isn't just confined to a certain age group but is available to anyone who will seek the Lord first in all he or she does. It's all about learning the lessons that God lays before you and applying that wisdom to your life. Giving your life to Christ means you also give Him your life's purpose. I refuse to just take up space in this world. I don't want anyone paying my vocational tithe for me. I want to take the life God has given me and make it count.

THE BOLDPRINT

YOU'RE MAKING MEMORIES. MAKE
THEM GOOD!

CHAPTER NINE

CREATIVE CHURCH IS BORN

Everyone has landmarks in their life. These are moments, events, or seasons that are meant to be unforgettable. They leave a mark on us whether we know it or not. Most people are on the basic cycle of life:

They are born.
They get an education.
They enter the work force.
They get into a routine.

They die.

While watching people's life over the last several years, I've noticed that we all sort of have seasonal patterns in our life. We are good for a while, and then we are not good. We tend to get into a cycle with our life.

It is in the grind of daily life that we usually allow pieces of our blueprint to fade away. A landmark from God for me was witnessing the birth of my children. What pivotal moments in your life brought you to the place you are? These landmarks can be good or bad. You may have gone through a bitter divorce. You may have lost a job at the worst time of your life. You may have won the lottery and then went bankrupt. Life is filled with moments that make us who we are.

Old relationships that were toxic, old habits and ways, or places you used to go can all be landmarks of death in our lives. You can hear a song that reignites a memory and suddenly you are taken to another place and time.

STONES OF REMEMBERANCE

In the book of Joshua, God raised up a new leader for Israel. Moses is dead and Joshua has been chosen by God to lead the people into the promised land. Before entering the new land, God will instruct Joshua to do a strange thing. Out of the twelve tribes of Israel Joshua is to select a representative from each tribe. This tribal leader will take a stone from the Jordan river and carry it over to the lodging place on the west side of the river. Each man will carry these stones upon their shoulder to the other side.

There will come a time when the children will ask their fathers "What do these stones mean?" The answer will be simple: they are landmarks from the Lord and what He did for His people. He parted the Red Sea and brought them out of slavery. Now, He has opened up the banks of the Jordan River. These stones will serve as a memorial or landmark for generations to come.

Joshua then sets up these rocks as an altar of remembrance. The nation will pass over to the plains of Jericho ready to take the land with these twelve stones stacked high as a living landmark of where they have been, where they are, and where they are going. I can almost see this in real time. In my mind, I can see families walking over the dry ground of the Jordan discussing the horrible memories of Egypt and the hope of a new life in the promise land. Did you know that just on the east side of the Jordan River is not the land of Egypt? However, to God, one step in the direction of Egypt is Egypt.

God used the Jordan River as a line of separation for his people. Never again would they have to go back toward the wilderness, the desert, or Egypt. God had set them free forever and was giving them a rocky reminder in the form of twelve stones. This was their landmark moment.

Guess what? You don't have to go back to your past life either!

What lines in the sand has God drawn for you?
What landmark moments has God sent your way?

If you can recognize the landmarks in your life and realize that God has placed a separation between you and your past, then you can march on toward your destiny. I can see the scene unfold in my mind as the children of Israel cross over the river. A child runs up to his father and asks "Daddy, what are those men carrying large rocks for?" The father takes his son past the pile of stones, turns around, looks behind them, and says "Son, these stones are a landmark and token from God. They remind us of what He has done! We don't have to ever go back to Egypt."

Have you ever been between a "rock and a hard spot"? Have you ever been to "rock bottom"?

These phrases are figures of speech that we often use to describe a dilemma. Just as God used the stones of the Jordan River, He uses the hard places of our life to remind us of the blessings of obedience and the curses of disobedience. Failing to see these landmarks can leave you lost on a page of your life. Don't miss the landmark moments.

TURN THE PAGE

In the fall of 2010, I was so tired of looking for a place to preach. I had been in ministry ten years and things felt as flat as a piece of paper. I felt like I had done nothing but be faithful, excel in the field God had placed me in, and bear fruit; yet, I was at a dead end. No one was really interested in having revivals with evangelists anymore. It wasn't cool to do a revival and that was the reality of things. The concept that many have of revival is a broad one and I realize that much of it can be good and some of it is not biblical.

Needless to say, I felt like I was always one or two paychecks away from being unemployed and I hated the constant battle of trying to provide for my family. Usually, people who want to say things like "well, just trust God" are usually not in the situation that you are currently in. Sometimes they haven't ever been in your situation.

I'm always interested in the thought pattern of people. I find it astounding that in the day that we live, people's emotions drive what the will of God seems to be. It's strange how some perceive it to be the will of God ONLY IF it profits them. Money becomes a measuring stick to see whether or not something is God's will. This is sad. I knew I was doing what God had called me to do.

It's easy to get into emotion when it comes to the will of God. But honestly, we need to seek God's blueprint before we pour any concrete. In 2010, I knew it was God's will for me to do what I was doing. The only problem was it certainly wasn't a financial wave of glory or anything close to it. We had two children at the time, and I was feeling the pressure of putting food in their mouth. I went into some intense examination of my life. God began to really deal with my heart about planting a church or even pastoring a church. I had never even thought about such a thing before. Honestly, my impression of most pastors wasn't a good one. Most pastors were frustrated and burned out with people.

Was it time to turn the page in my life?

In the late fall of 2010, I was contacted by a church to come and consider being their pastor. I flew down and interviewed. I ministered to the church on that particular Sunday and things went well. Lindsey and I prayed about the situation and had peace about the proposal of becoming lead pastor. A few weeks later, we were stunned to realize that the leadership of that denomination had stepped in and removed me as a viable option for the church to consider.

Just like that…it was over.

We flew home. For a few days, we simply sat looking across the table at each other.

"What are we going to do now?" Lindsey asked me.

"I don't know, but I'm going to pray, or at least try to pray," I responded.

I gathered myself just enough to not get bitter, but I sure wanted to be mad, sad, or something similar. I was hurt and hurt bad. My heart was broken and so was my checking account. I was very discouraged, beaten, and just spiritually lost.

I had given my life to the call of God and where had it gotten me? I felt like God was almost picking on me. I don't remember how many days or weeks it was after this that I was in our living room and I was talking to God.

"Lord, what do you want me to do now?" I cried out.

Silence.

A few minutes went by and it seemed like the Lord sat down beside me.

"Go and build what I have put inside of you."

It was like ten years of pain, trials, and miles converged in that prayer moment with God.

LIVIN' ON A PRAYER

In 2004, Lindsey and I were married. She traveled with me as I preached all around the southeast. We were preaching near Savannah, Georgia once and decided to take our time to travel up the coastal highways of the Carolinas. It was our off day and we were traveling from one revival up to another one. We were riding with the windows down singing Bon Jovi's "Livin' on a Prayer" and the song title wasn't far from being the complete truth and reality! We stopped in Savannah, Georgia and Charleston, South Carolina. We traveled up the coastal scenic highways. Suddenly I looked over at Lindsey and said "One day we are going to be here. One day, we will live here."

She replied, "What? What makes you say that?"

I replied, "I don't know. I'm just telling you that one day, we are going to live here or be spiritually connected somehow here in this area. I just feel it!"

As I was driving along, something seemed to just quicken this thought on the inside of me.

In the fall of 2010, the scene of us driving through the low country of Carolina came up before my eyes. I could literally see inside of my spirit as Lindsey and I were back in that car driving along and singing out loud. I knew God was speaking to me to go and build what he had placed inside of me. So, later that year, I wrote the vision of what I would call Creative Church. After traveling for ten years and preaching in countless churches, what had I learned? What would this vision look like?

I had no funds. I had no denominational approval. I had no Plan B. Plan B was to make Plan A work! I contacted a few ministry friends and talked to them about considering investing in my dream called Creative Church. I raised $3,000 on my own and Lindsey shared with her family the news that we would be relocating.

In January 2011, we launched Creative Church in a hotel conference room. You heard me right!! We rented a small conference room at a hotel located in Bluffton, South Carolina and we had our first service. At that service there were about twenty-five people in attendance. The next Sunday, we had about fourteen people. The following Sunday, we had about eight or ten. The next Sunday, there was no one there except Lindsey, the two kids, and me. I chuckled within myself "This is going wonderful." A week later, Lindsey's grandfather passed away. A few weeks later, we had lost every single person that we launched with originally. I thought, "Did I miss something?"

I felt like the plinko chip on the *Price is Right* (Sandler, 2011). I had been thrown down the board of life and was bouncing off of each metal pole until I landed in a slot. I felt like I was dangling somewhere between God's providence and His sovereignty. It was exciting but it wasn't anything pretty, to say the least. Nevertheless, Lindsey and I kept moving forward.

AN UNFINISHED DREAM

After ten months of meeting as a church in a hotel conference room, we moved into a building across from the local college. The building was located near a growing part of the community. The building would seat about two hundred people and allow us to grow. We stayed there a few years and then something incredible happened. Before I take you forward, let me take you back.

In 2004, a church, Abundant Life, located in Hardeeville, South Carolina, was experiencing incredible heartbreak. Their pastor,

107

Charles Bowman had passed away after a long and hard fight with cancer. For over thirty-five years, he had stood strong as a spiritual leader in their community. He was deeply loved by many. From 2004 on, Abundant Life went through great struggle and decreased as a body until only a handful of the body of believers remained. In the summer of 2015, a few of the remaining members came over to Creative Church after Abundant Life closed.

Keep in mind that in the same year as Pastor Bowman was going to Heaven, Lindsey and I were preparing to get married. Eleven years later, the remaining members of his beloved church Abundant Life, found new life at Creative Church. In 2015, one of those remaining members came to me with Pastor Bowman's son, Barry, and said, "Pastor Eric, Abundant Life Church and property is for sale. Would you want to try to buy it?" I was hesitant at first out of fear. Yet, we as a small church, made a big leap and bought the entire property. We moved in and purchased new air units, painted, cleaned up, and had our first service in the summer of 2015. We own 13.4 acres and a facility that currently seats about 900, feeds the hungry, ministers to the community, and houses hundreds of believers on a weekly basis. The dream that Pastor Bowman had forty years prior was still alive! The tree had been cut down, but the root was still good! Currently Creative Church is an ever-growing body of believers with every color of skin!

Now, are these things just coincidence? I don't think so. God knew what was coming down the road.

"PLAN B" IS TO MAKE "PLAN A" WORK!

CHAPTER TEN
COINCIDENCE OR PROVIDENCE

If it were possible for you to live across time and across all ages and then to chronicle all that had happened in your life, would your life bore people with monotony, shock them, or would they simply be unmoved? Most of the people that are in your life right now came into your life in the middle of all the madness of life. It's similar to someone walking into a movie after the movie has already started. They are immediately lost as to the narrative and they usually ask countless questions. This is the way our lives are. People are coming in and out of our lives now, more than ever, at a rapid pace. Technology has broadened our relationship avenues but also eliminated the time required for true relationship to take roots. We are instant friends or instant enemies. We don't take time to really get to know people. People walk into our lives, and vice versa, and have no idea the scenes that have already unfolded. They see the current scene. The mud of the past has long dried and the pain of yesterday is only felt by you and you alone.

I THINK I'M CALLED TO PREACH... I THINK.

Your life is the result of three things. **First, you are the result of the power of decision**. Whether your choices are right or wrong they are still yours to decide. Choices often can be tough to make. Hard choices are often set up by God to shape our destiny and us. **Secondly, you are who you are because of the decisions of others.** You could not choose your parents, or your portion in this life as a child. Some things in this life we cannot control. **Lastly, you are a result of the providence of God.**

So, what is the providence of God?

Let me explain it through telling you a story.

My first memory of church is a Sunday school room where an older woman was teaching the Bible. It was here that in the early 80's our church hosted what was called a "revival." The evangelist's name was Brett Cooper. I remember it was a rainy night and my grandmother took me to revival that night. I was very young, and I could not sit still in church. This was long before ADD or any other disorders were commonly known. My grandmother told me to lay down and take a nap on the pew. I remember it was near the back of the church. Brett Cooper took the pulpit to minister and I woke up. I woke up and stood there in awe. My head didn't stick much higher than the back of the pew. A voice then seemed to whisper to me "This is what you will do one day." Of course, I didn't run out of the door and become an evangelist that night. The seed that was planted there would emerge over time. Yet, that night, something deep in my heart shook me and would not let go.

I didn't attend Bible school. I didn't receive a prophesy from any prophet. I had no special, specific training to be a preacher. *I was just a boy with a dream.* I had this intangible determination that I was going to be somebody in life. I am that same dreamer to this day! The night my grandmother took me to revival, I wasn't fully aware, nor did I have total understanding of what God was doing in my heart.

In high school, I had a teacher that would call my house and say "Eric, get up and get to school. You are not going to be a failure. You are going to graduate." She was the reason I did…graduate. I, then, went to college and that lasted all of two semesters. At this point, I was an aimless and hopeless teenager with zero direction or drive to succeed. I really didn't know how to succeed. How in the world do you just become a preacher and live happily ever after? I had no idea what I wanted to do with my life.

I went to my pastor and said, "I feel like I am called to preach." He gave me sound advice. "Eric, many evangelists are starving to death. Are you sure this is what you want to do?" I responded, "I think so." So off I went into the field of preaching.

In 2003, I was preaching in north Alabama. We were in our third week of revival and I needed a break. I drove down to Pensacola, Florida to the Brownsville Revival. I had never been there before, so I just went for a service. Jentezen Franklin preached that night. I sat there thinking, "Wow, can he preach!". I saw this beautiful girl there that night. Her name was Lindsey, and, in the summer of 2004, I married her.

Now, I didn't plan any of the events that I just told you about. I didn't plan where Creative Church would be planted. After a season of rejection in 2010, I literally asked God, "Where do you want this work to be planted?" All of this happened according to God's providence. God put the pieces in place. Who would have dreamed that in 2004 as a church was dying in Hardeeville, South Carolina that another church would be planted in 2011 engrafting the remaining branches of that work that Pastor Bowman had planted, bringing forth an incredible tree of life? A miracle indeed! The evangelist, Brett Cooper, that preached revivals at the church I attended when I was a kid is now preaching revivals for me at Creative Church. God, in His providence, brings things full circle.

We all have our own story to tell. My story is just a string of events that the world would call coincidence. God calls these things *providence.*

"We may throw the dice, but the Lord determines how they fall." **Proverbs 16:33, New Living Translation**

Don't gamble with God, He will win! He knows the future including *your* future!

The world has terms like premonition, serendipity, and coincidence. God has His timing and His way. He calls it providence.

My childhood was a part of God's providence.

Brett Cooper was a part of God's providence.

Meeting Lindsey was a part of God's providence.

Abundant Life and Pastor Bowman were a part of God's providence.

Creative Church was a part of God's providence.

You.... yes, YOU are a part of God's providence.

WHAT'S YOUR STORY?

Have you ever considered how powerful your story really is? We all were slaves to sin and self. Everyone has a slave story! It's not just the coincidences of life that brought you to this point. I'm certainly not suggesting that the God of the Bible has brought everything into your life, but I am saying that God knows exactly where you have come from and nothing has to be wasted in Him. When the grace of God gets on a situation, it serves as a marinade that softens our hearts and allows God to get glory out of our life. Ultimately, there is no real loss when the grace of Jesus is present! Your slave story becomes your life story when God gets involved. Let Him take the ashes of yesterday and build a story that touches others!

Do all things work together for the good for everyone? No. All things are working together for the good of those that love God. God is at work in our lives. For the sinner, they have no covenant with God. They are living under mercy. For the believer in Jesus, they are living under *grace* and mercy. The blood of Jesus is the ink that signed the check for their freedom!

The household of faith has the advantage! God is working like a master tailor pulling the strings of their life together. The Lord orders the steps of a good man. Things that we face that seem as if they are debilitating often times end up setting up the posts and pillars that our biggest blessings are built upon. Look back at every burning bush now and see if you can see the God of grace holding back the hands of death at different times. Guess what! The moments of God's mercy that you remember are not really the only ones. Those are just the ones you remember. I believe God often spares us from all types of situations that we are never aware of. Your story isn't over yet and God is still working on the details!

A DREAM AND A MAP

In Acts 16, Paul and Silas were preaching throughout Galatia and Asia and many people were being saved on a regular basis. They came through two cities, Derbe and Lystra. From here they went on to Phrygia and throughout the region of Galatia. It's here that the Bible says:

"Now when they had gone throughout Phrygia and the region of Galatia, and were forbidden of the Holy Ghost to preach the word in Asia, After they were come to Mysia, they assayed to go into Bithynia: but the Spirit suffered them not."
Acts 16:6, King James Version

This is incredible. The Holy Ghost said no to a good thing- the gospel. Is that possible? It happened here in this text. God will stop you from the good things to get you to the God things. The Holy Spirit stopped them from going north to Bithynia (modern day Turkey), and instead they traveled west to Troas. Troas sat on the coast of the Aegean Sea. During the night Paul had a dream or vision. In this vision, he saw a man standing across the sea in Macedonia pleading with him to come to Macedonia and help them. Paul woke up and was shaken by the dream. Literally, a dream from the Lord changed his entire direction in life. A dream from the Lord gave him a map! A dream from the Lord will give you direction, as well.

Scripture says in **Acts 16:10, New International Version** "After Paul had seen the vision, we got ready at once to leave for Macedonia, concluding that God had called us to preach the gospel to them."

Paul now knew why the Lord had blocked his way north. It was simply because He wanted him to travel west into another area to preach the gospel. They set loose from Troas and sailed for Macedonia. After landing, they ended up in Philippi and on the Sabbath went down to a prayer meeting at the river. There, they met a woman named Lydia, who was a believer.

Paul and Silas, who were accustomed to evangelizing a city, were now evangelizing one person outside the city down by the river. The rabbis of old times would say "Better the law be burnt, than delivered to a woman." Yet, the plan of God is no respecter of gender, preference, or color. The Bible says that the Lord had "opened her heart." Lydia was baptized and her household and she entreated Paul and his ministry team to lodge at her house that night. Along the way, Paul dealt with a demon-possessed slave girl, who was a fortune-teller and earned much money for her masters. He cast the demon out of the young girl. The only problem was that her masters saw that their money stream was now cut off. So, they seized Paul and Silas and brought them to the rulers of the city and in the midst of a fiery mob, they were beaten and thrown in jail.

JAIL BIRDS

All these facts, twists, and turns seem coincidental, but they're not! Something is going to happen in this jail that very night that would change the course of everyone's life. Midnight came and Paul and Silas began to sing praises unto God. I have known and read this story for a long time and it seems to blossom every time I read it again.

At midnight, when men ought to be sleeping, these two men went into robust praise to God.

Are you spiritually asleep when you ought to be spiritually singing praise?

At midnight, when one day is ending and a new one is beginning?

Are you in transition in life and need direction?

At midnight when it seems the darkest, the light of God's supernatural power flooded in.

Does life seem to be as dark as midnight? Good, it's time

for a miracle.

At midnight, as the songs of praise left the lips of these two men, suddenly there was an earthquake. The foundations of the prison were shaken, the doors flew open, and every prisoner's chains fell off their hands and feet. Notice when the two servants of the Lord got free, everyone else got free as well. It was a domino effect of God's providence!

JUST FOR ONE

When the lead jailor burst in and saw all the doors of the prison open, he assumed the worst. Pulling his sword, he was about to kill himself.

Stop at this scene in your mind for just one moment.

I don't know where you live, but I know where I live, and in this nation, the plague of death that seems to have gripped people is quite astonishing. This suicidal spirit that has attached itself to our culture doesn't just come for one color or one age bracket. It has come for us all. The church must break this demonic spirit. How though? We must stand in resistance to it. We must preach the whole gospel at every one of our gathered assemblies. We must get out of the *Sunday* mentality and be salt and light from Monday to Saturday as well. We must provide an atmosphere of life, hope, and comfort for those outside the body of Christ. If we stand in opposition to death, we must also participate in the ministry of life. This includes: mentoring, volunteering, counseling, adoption, foster care, or perhaps the greatest strength of all- being willing to HELP should any situation arise from this suicidal wave.

Paul screams out, "Don't do that! We're all still here! Nobody's run away!" **Acts 16:28, The Message Translation**
This should be the battle cry of our Christian assemblies, congregations, youth groups, and all believers. **We are all here WITH YOU IN THE FIGHT!**

The miracle of this story is in how it ends. The jailor stands in the midst of them all and says to Paul and Silas, "What do I need to do to be saved?" They told him, "Believe on the Lord Jesus Christ and you will be saved and your entire family, as well."

The Lord had brought Paul west for at least two people- Lydia and this jailor. Is providence that detailed and specific? Yes, yes, it is! That night the jailor took Paul and Silas into this house and washed and cleaned their wounds. The man who had ordered them to be beaten, or who had beaten them himself, was now their nurse! This man's entire house was born again through the strange providence of God.

I don't know what became of this jailor, but I would bet God used him mightily. The world would call all this stuff pure coincidence, but God calls it providence. It's when God is pulling the strings of all situations for the greater glory of His Kingdom and the greater good of His child.

This was incredible providence for just one person! God loves them all and loves the one all the same!

Fate, fortune, and luck have nothing to do with your destiny. The providence of God includes everything large and small in our lives, including God's dealings with mankind. God is bringing the entire cosmos to one moment when it will be subject to His reign forever. He will make His enemies His footstool and yet, He knows the exact number of hairs on your head. God controls all things for the highest good of the whole. Nothing is really small with God!

THE BOLDPRINT

> **THE MASTER TAILOR IS PULLING THE STRINGS OF YOUR LIFE TOGETHER.**

CHAPTER ELEVEN
MAY I TAKE YOUR ORDER

Don't live life at random. I know that doesn't sound like the most popular thing you've heard lately but it's true. The thing that prayer and life itself have in common is that we rarely do either. We rarely pray and spend time with God. We rarely live life without unnecessary stresses, worry, and a fear of things that usually never come to pass. We often simply exist.

I know people that believe that life should just be spontaneous and without any plumb lines to guide us. Yet, spontaneity flows from disciplines. The price of wisdom is discipline.

You have to ask to receive.

You must seek in order to find.

You must knock if you want the door to be opened.

122

Consistent prayer is the basis for answered prayer. The Kingdom of God is moved by fervency!

It is the discipline of prayer that makes possible those exceptional times of free communication with God. Life is the same way. Unless you order something, you will starve. The steps of a good man are ordered by the Lord. If life seems empty, it may be because you are not ordering anything. Choosing to not pray is like starving to death while sitting in a grocery store.

The mouth, specifically the tongue, is the hinge on which the door of your life swings. From the tongue proceed blessing and cursing. Are you telling the members of the body what to do in the name of the Lord? Are you telling your feet where to go and your eyes what they'll see? Are you ordering the day that God has given you?

I have four children at home. One thing I have learned about children is that a large part of their development has to do with what we are placing in their spiritual diet. Are we provoking them to love or wrath? We should be speaking to our children concerning God's blueprint for their life. We shouldn't be embracing and receiving disorder, we should be embracing God's plan and His order over the lives of our children.

When Adam fell in the garden, everything fell with him. The whole creation awaits God's proper order and the return of the Son of God. Until then, if you don't put your life in order, something else will. If you don't make your schedule, the devil will.

I THINK I JUST ATE A WHALE

Jesus said, "He that believeth on me, as the scripture hath said, out of his belly shall flow rivers of living water."
John 7:38, King James Version

What was Jesus talking about here in this verse? He was talking specifically about the person of the Holy Spirit. That same person, the Holy Spirit, comes to lead us into all truth, convict us, comfort us, and to reveal unto us the deepest desires of the Father. The Holy Spirit reveals the deepest desires of our heart as well.

Every man is born with a spirit. Though we are born lost, we are born with a human spirit. That human spirit is alive and will be developed over time. I've met people with a mean spirit, and I've met people with a kind spirit. Usually what determines this is what the individual has done with the let-downs of life. Trouble happens to us all, but it's what we do with that trouble that creates a strong spirit or a wounded spirit.

Our human spirit is like a small trickle of water. That trickle begins to flow, and a stream emerges. Usually in our teens, that stream becomes a creek and then a river! We don't fully understand our human spirit until we are born again. Our spirit is a river of death until we are born again, and then suddenly our

124

spirit comes alive.

If I were to die tomorrow, my biggest bother wouldn't be missed time with family, that I didn't make enough money, or that I had things left on my bucket list. It would simply be-that's it? I'm done? My spirit would leap within screaming "I am not done yet! I am not finished with the work that God placed deep inside of my spirit."

Inside the heart of every human being is a lion that hasn't roared, a king or queen uncrowned, or a dreamer awakened too soon, or never awakened at all.

When you are lost and alienated from the life of God, you are like the prophet, Jonah. As Jonah ran from God, so are you. You may not feel discontent, frustrated, or lost but according to God's word-you ARE lost. You may feel like you're on top of the world. Well, you may be, but you are made batteries sold separately. God placed a space deep inside of you that only He can fill.

Jonah was on the wrong ship going to the wrong place. He was in rebellion. So, guess what! God prepared a whale to swallow Jonah. God anointed a whale to take him on a journey and God has selected a whale to take you on a journey too. The whale won't vomit you up until you truly repent and come clean with God. Now, for the child of God, we don't get eaten by the whale, but rather we get to eat the whale. Anyone who has ever done anything, small or big, for God comes to a point where they begin to see the whale inside of them. Our inner whale grows as we feed it with the fruits of the Spirit. Your whale is the plan of God for your life. Call it your purpose, your call, your destiny, or whatever you want to call it. Most people are bloated with life and never truly come to a place where their inner whale comes to life. As we pray and walk in obedience, God will bring His dreams inside of us to pass.

YOU CAN'T JUDGE A BOOK

Each person's life is like a book. Some men pen their own autobiography by living a life of self. The end result is a novel of death. Others allow Almighty God to pen their life upon the pages of time. God fashions and molds us to His liking. The person who carves out his own way usually cuts slices into his hands. In the book of Revelation, the writer John saw books that were opened before the throne of God. He saw another book opened which was called *The Book of Life*. Our lives are like a book that is full of wins, losses, victories, and defeats.

The really good books tend to get overlooked. For the most part, they don't have a fancy cover and to the human eye, they aren't worth reading. Yet, these are the lives that usually contain pure wisdom and life changing advice! I hear people say, "I'm living the good life." Well, I don't know if I'm living the good life, but I am living the *full* life. Our lives are full of joy, sadness, blessings, and bruises!

Remember, don't quit in one chapter of your life. Never get so down on one page of your life that you can't see the joy of the next page in life. In Revelation 5, John sees seven scrolls or books that are locked with a seal. John wondered who would open the scrolls. No one in Heaven or Earth seemed to be found worthy to open them and reveal their content. Just as all hope seemed lost, the elder in John's vision cried aloud, "Weep not: behold, the Lion of the tribe of Juda, the Root of David, hath prevailed to open the book, and loose the seven seals thereof." **Revelation 5:5, King James Version**

If life is a book, then no one can open that book except the author. Jesus Christ can open your life and take the pages where hurt was penned down and turn them into letters of victory. He will take the damaged places and heal them. He will change the plot, characters, and bring a glorious story to light.

DAYDREAM BELIEVERS

Dreams and their interpretations are a hot topic in our culture. The world, at large, loves the idea of the supernatural and spirit world; however, the dream I'm talking about is not a dream you have because you ate too much one night, seemed restless, or woke up in a panic. The dreams I'm talking about are not necessarily night visions of things to come. There is another type of dream-the kind you have with your eyes open.

The devil can put a dream in your heart. Yes, it's true. One way to know that it is of the enemy is how little it involves others.

Joseph dreamed a dream, and, in his dream, he saw a harvest field. The dreams that God gives are dreams that bring Him glory and may or may not be exactly what your flesh had in mind. The enemy will give you a dream to satisfy your flesh but when the dream comes to pass, you wake up realizing your life was wasted. God's will for your life above, and well above, any other thing in your life is that you are saved. If you are not saved, you are living your own dream, not the dreams that God desires. Again, one way to know if your dream is of God is to ask yourself, "Does this bring God glory, or does it bring me glory?"

The devil shouts.
God whispers.

The devil will pressurize you into his will. God will lead you into His will. If the devil can't slow you down, then he will try to speed you up!

Whenever God writes His dream inside of your heart, it will linger in your heart. This *lingering* is God's way of getting you to pray about it. How will you know it's God? The dream will become stronger and stronger. God expands your hopes and draws you into a new realm of faith. Suddenly, you go from a *just get by* mentality to an "I can do all things through Christ" mentality. Maybe you are reading this from a place of famine. Perhaps you live in just a small place and you have children. Maybe, the place you are in is not adequate for you and your family. Maybe your dream is that God would give you your own home. It would be a brick home with a big yard for your children. Can you see it?

Winston Churchill said, "A man can't be great unless he or she lives in a great country, lives in a great time, and accomplishes great things." Mr. Churchill was sincere, but he was sincerely wrong. Jesus lived in a very insignificant country that was ruled by the Roman empire, and yet He changed the world. Jesus Christ is the reason we have a calendar. All of time changed because of Him. You don't have to fall into anyone's boundaries and expectations. The Bible teaches us to open our mouth wide and God will fill it. In order for our dreams to come to pass, we must be persistent in prayer and mean business with God. Don't stop dreaming. Rather, open up your eyes and keep dreaming!

I JUST KNEW

The first three years of pastoring Creative Church, for me, was similar to being the new animal at the zoo. I just sort of did whatever I could do to be spiritual, draw people, and not starve to death. It was only after an encounter with God in 2015 that God began to show me some things about pastoring. For three and half years I had been their preacher. Now I was going to be their pastor. I don't want you to think this just happened overnight. Over the next several years, God would give me the grace to pastor people. It seemed as though I was stepping into my own skin. I had never been a pastor and had no desire to be one. I was an evangelist and that's what I knew.

The call of God is personal, but not without mystery. I didn't really know why I had to plant a church, I just knew that's what I was supposed to do. I didn't really understand the details of relocating my family to a place I was unfamiliar with, but I knew I had to.

I hear people talk about church attendance as if it is a choice they have. God determines where we go to church, not us. You may not be completely comfortable about the church God has planted you in. In fact, if you are always comfortable, you are probably in the wrong church. God will plant you where you are comforted, challenged, convicted, and growing. You may not know the full set of reasons why you attend, you will just know that you have to! God doesn't work well with complacency. Only that which is planted will bring forth fruit. Stay planted!

I get the question from time to time, "When did you know or decide to be a preacher?"

My answer is always the same. "I tried to do other things, but I knew deep within my heart that this is what I had to do." I didn't come out of the womb with a career list that had minister written anywhere on it. I remember being a kid thinking "I must preach," and not really knowing why. I can't explain it, but I just knew my destiny was simple-preach Jesus and lift Him higher. Can you see me as a car salesman or an insurance salesman? Me neither.

THE BOLDPRINT

OPEN YOUR EYES AND KEEP DREAMING!

CHAPTER 12
RIGHT PLACE. RIGHT PERSON. RIGHT TIME

For nearly forty years, God rained down manna from Heaven on the nation of Israel. After their exodus, they were miraculously fed in the wilderness by the manna. God provided for them on a daily basis.

"And the manna ceased on the morrow after they had eaten of the children of Israel manna anymore; but they did eat of the fruit of the land of Canaan that year." **Joshua 5:12, King James Version**

Think about that verse for just a moment. God literally let it rain bread every single day for nearly forty years. Psalms 78 tells us that God commanded the clouds and opened **the doors of**

Heaven. The Bible refers to this manna as the "corn of Heaven."

Man did eat angels' food. Though the Hebrew people were living in tents in a wilderness, God sent them meat to the full.

DOORS AND WINDOWS

Throughout the scripture, we see the concept of *doors and windows*. What do I mean? In the account of Noah and the ark, the scripture says that God opened the fountains of the great deep and also **the windows of Heaven**. In the book of Malachi, a few of the themes are offerings, money, and the tithe. We are told that if they would bring all the tithes to the storehouse that the Lord would open to them **the windows of Heaven** and pour out a blessing that would be overwhelming.

These two windows are very different. The first set were windows of judgement. The second set of windows were windows of blessing. In case you're wondering, you want the windows of blessings, not the windows of judgement.

The apostle Paul spoke many times of different *doors* that God had opened for him. They were doors of the gospel and opportunity for that gospel to go forth. He talked about a **"great door"** (See I Corinthians 16:9, King James Version). A great door is a door that opens to you as you approach it. You must take the steps in faith in order to see these great doors open. These are doors that God places before us that swing wide open even though there are adversaries.

Then, there were *"doors of faith"* (See Acts 14:27 King James Version). Paul rehearsed his first missionary journey to all those who had gathered around. He spoke to them about how God had opened "the door of faith" unto the Gentiles. A door of faith seems to be when the surge of faith has come into our lives and has risen up in our spirit. A door of faith is when you just feel your faith rise for a specific assignment or need. Yes, sometimes you can *feel* your faith!

Then Paul spoke about *"a door of utterance"* to speak the mystery of Christ (See Colossians 4:3, King James Version). Did you know your mouth is a door? God gave us sixty-six books in the library of the Bible to place His promises in our mouth. Often times we speak the Word of God and believe His great promises and then we see no changes for the good. So, what we usually do is lock the door of utterance or we begin to allow things to come out of our mouth that is not of faith.

These doors that Paul spoke about are directly connected to the gospel of Jesus Christ. God is not just interested in opening doors for you for your sake alone.

God opens doors for you *and* Him. If God has opened *a door* for you and your family then walk through that door, just take Jesus with you!

There is another window and door in Luke 5 that you need to

know about. Here Jesus withdrew himself into the wilderness and prayed.

"And it came to pass on a certain day, as he was teaching, that there were Pharisees and doctors of the law sitting by, which were come out of every town of Galilee, and Judaea, and Jerusalem: and *the power of the Lord was present* to heal them." **Luke 5:17, King James Version**

This is strange language to me. Was this *power* exclusive to only this moment? Did this mean it wasn't present before or wouldn't be present after? Countless people were healed after this moment and miracles were happening before this moment, as well. As Jesus came from the wilderness of prayer, something unique was happening in His life. I realize that some will call this silly, but clearly the writer is trying to tell us of a door of Heaven that was opened. I don't think He had a *better* anointing after praying in the wilderness but rather a *different* anointing. Jesus came into the city in the power of the Spirit.

The power of the Lord was present. The door of healing and miracles was open, and it was open wide! God had opened the front gate to the garden, so to speak! This unusual anointing that was upon Jesus was noted by those who were there as they shouted, "We have seen strange things today." They were amazed.

POWER IN TWO REALMS

Jesus recognized the windows of Heaven were opened! In this story (Luke 5) they brought a man who was confined to a cot or bed due to palsy. As the man was let down through the tiling of the roof on a cot, Jesus saw their faith and forgave the crippled man for his sins.

What did I just say?

I thought he came to get healed? He did. Yet, the power of the Lord was present to heal every area of his life. That same power is still present to heal every area of our lives as well.

Jesus spoke to two realms in this story when He forgave him of his sins and healed him of his infirmity. He told the young man to rise up, take his mat, and go home. The power of the Lord was present to heal his spiritual issue and his physical problem as well! This man got two healings for the price of one! Jesus never touched the crippled man and the man never touched Him as far as we know. Healing was in the atmosphere to be claimed by anyone through faith. The men that brought the crippled man had already reached out in faith unto God. They had the raw sincere faith to believe that if they loaded him up and carried him to this house in Capernaum of Galilee that perhaps Jesus would grant him a miracle.

It worked too.

Yet, their faith didn't stop when they arrived. They arrived and a massive crowd was in and surrounding the house where Jesus was. So, plan B is to make plan A work! They had the audacious faith to find a way to the top of the house, remove the tiling, and lower their friend to Jesus. When the power of the Lord is present, we ought to be quite bold in our approach to Jesus. This young man truly received a double portion miracle.

THE ROCK BESIDE HIM

"…for there shall no man see me, and live." **Exodus 33:20 (b), King James Version**

These were the words God told Moses. There was no option to see the full glory of God for Moses, but God gave him a second option. What was that? There was a place God had on reserve. A place Moses could get in that he could find the strength and wisdom he needed to lead the people through the wilderness. They were rebellious, stubborn, and complaining to Moses on a daily basis. God told him "***There is a place beside me.***" That place beside God was and literally is "Christ our Rock" and cornerstone of our faith.

"God said, 'Look, here is a place right beside me. Put yourself on this rock. When my Glory passes by, I'll put you in the cleft of the rock and cover you with my hand until I've passed by. Then I'll take my hand away and you'll see my back. But you won't see my face.'" **Exodus 33: 21-23, The Message**

Have you ever witnessed a basketball player in a game make a shot or two and then he gets what we call a *hot hand*? He hits three or four shots in a row and his confidence rises. His teammates look at him and say "Man, you're on fire!" It's as though he can't miss a shot! We call this the sweet spot. What you see in Exodus 33 verse 21-23 is the sweet spot of God.

Every season isn't good.
Every situation isn't good.
Every person isn't good.
Everything isn't good.

Yet, God is good. If you will be faithful, you will see all things working together for your good!

Life isn't always fair, but my faith in Christ has grown to the point where, at different times, I have felt like I was standing on this rock beside God. You don't get here by being a better Christian. Growth doesn't come through striving with God, but rather surrendering to Him. It's a place of grace. Enabling grace is found in this place beside God. Moses would lay in the cleft of this mysterious rock and God would pass by Him in the fullness of His glory. The crevice of this rock was Christ Himself.

The opening of the rock, Christ Himself, is our foundation of everything we believe. Just as Moses stood with two feet in the crevice of this rock, we also stand with our own feet in the bloody footprints of Jesus and by His grace WE STAND! Stand ON Christ. Stand WITH Christ. Stand FOR Christ.

When we stand on the rock beside God, we can swing in the game of life and expect to hit the ball. There are those that teach that we are supposed to experience constant pain, sorrow, and trials. I do believe in this life we will have to contend with the enemy. Life, with or without a devil, is full of mountains. Yet, we are not supposed to expect defeat! Should we plan to fail? No. God knows what lessons are going to press our limits and He knows we will need grace indefinitely. We are supposed to pray, believe, and receive. Jesus Himself instituted a method to which we are to approach the King and the Kingdom. We are supposed to ask to receive, seek to find, and knock to see the doors open. That's faith!

God can put you in the sweet spot! Yes, He can!

The sweet spot seems to be when we come to the right place at the right time. Often times, the sweet spot is preceded by a sour spot. Your greatest accomplishment in life may be the simple fact that you would not quit. Don't give up.

UNTIL THE TIME

Think about Joseph. He was seventeen years old when God gave him a dream that would affect him and his entire generation. The next thing that happens to him is he is sold into slavery. He ends up in Egypt and eventually in prison for crimes he did not commit. There he stayed in prison for at least two years. Do you think he felt like God had a *divine blueprint* while sitting in that prison? Hardly. He felt like the poster child for "I missed the plan of God."

Joseph, no doubt, felt as if he had missed the will of God entirely. He hadn't.

Nothing is more dangerous than a child of God (the right person), with the Word of God (the will of God), walking in the right season (the right place) with God.

"But he had already sent a man ahead of his people to Egypt; it was Joseph, who was sold as a slave. His feet were bruised by strong shackles and his soul was held by iron. God's promise to Joseph purged his character **until it was time for his dreams to come true**. Eventually, the king of Egypt sent for him, setting him free at last. Then Joseph was put in charge of everything under the king; he became the master of the palace over all of the royal possessions." **Psalms 105:17-21, The Passion Translation**

It was a complete miracle!! Who just walks out of prison? The only thing that was certain is that Joseph would not be a prisoner one moment past God's providence in his life. Joseph's word, the word that God had given him through dreams, was ready to come alive. It was moving day for him! He was moving out of prison and into the blueprint God had for him. He was about to save an entire nation and his own family who had sold him years ago. Through the providence of God, the plan was unveiled and had come to full fruition!

THE BOLDPRINT

GET THROUGH THE SOUR.
THE SWEET IS COMING!

CHAPTER 13
CORKBOARD DREAMS

You have a heart to love, a will to choose, and a mind to think. This is what makes you uniquely different from the animal kingdom. You're not a monkey, whale, or a dog! You not only *have* a soul, but you *are* a soul.

Predestination, simply put, is the fact that God predestined all of this before time began and we are simply marching to the beat of His drum. The first book of the Bible, literally on page one, gives us the entire answer to the debate of human choices vs. predestination. "And God said, let us make man in our image, after our likeness…" **Genesis 1:26 (a), King James Version**

There you have it. God created man in His image. Before Jesus Christ came to this earth, we see God in the beginning, and throughout the Old Testament time, on the move! How? God moved through creation, laws, miracles, governments, and judgements. The Spirit of God has been moving across the earth in a creative fashion since God formed the entire cosmos. Nothing has changed!

We aren't little gods. We are males or females. We are made a little lower than the angels. Now, in the Old Testament we see God is moving. Do we move? We see, throughout the Bible, and history God speaking to humanity. Do we speak? We see throughout all of time God making and carrying out decisions. Do we do the same? Yes, of course!

THE VOICE OF CHOICE

Choices are a big deal. Choices become the quick sand or solid ground that we build our life upon. We are God's highest form of creation here on Earth, created in His image, we have the power to choose. The Bible represents man as a reasonable creature having the faculty of contriving for himself. A person's heart devises his way, designs an end, and projects a way leading to that end. Even as terrible and low as our society has sank, we still attempt to hold people responsible for their choices. Every man's conscience testifies to the fact that he has the power to make his own choices. Chance, fate, and fortune are words without substance. You are the result of a choice and you, yourself, make choices. In God's sovereignty, there is a heaven and there is a hell. In man's choice he chooses one or the other.

Our decisions determine our destiny; short for destination!

We have the ability to think like we want, act like we want, talk like we want, and live just as we so desire. If we were creatures of force, then we could never experience remorse. There would be no need for the sting of the conscience against anything wrong, and why repent if we can't help it anyway? One of God's primary witnesses inside the human spirit is the conscience. Living life without believing that God gave you the right to choose is living life without compass or chart. If you desire to live the full life and have the freedom to sail the seas of life, then go ahead and take the chart and compass with you. We make choices and God blesses us or chastens us accordingly. So, what's the good news?

If you are saved, then you are His redeemed child. He doesn't correct you as a stranger, but as a child. He deals with us as children, not slaves.

Genetics tell us that we are the sons and daughters of Adam, the first man.

Jesus gives us the opportunity for this to not be the final Adam in our life! Jesus is the second Adam bringing life to all of those who will believe!

SOVEREIGN

There are a series of events that lead you to where you are right now. Whether "right now" is what you want it to be or not, it's the present reality. There's a big word in the Bible world called *sovereignty*. In short, what it means is that God possesses all power, is supreme, and has all authority to the point that He is in control and can accomplish whatsoever He pleases.

Now, you are probably thinking "Didn't you just tell us that our choices determine our destiny?"

Yes, it's true. God does have control over all. It's also true that we are creatures made in the image of God with the ability to choose. Can both cases be a true factor in human affairs? Well, of course. Life is what happens as we are caught in the middle of God's sovereignty (God's purposes) and man's choice (man's will).

God works all things after the counsel of His own purposes and will. Does man always do God's will? No, but God's purposes are still performed. Adam and Eve didn't do God's will, but God's purposes were still performed. In God's sovereignty, there was a lamb slain for man's sin before the foundation of the world. We can't fully explain, and no one else can either, why evil was even permitted. Yet, God overrules it to the good. All things will come to reveal the final purposes of God. Even the origin of sin has revealed to us the mercy and love of God.

The ability we have to choose is like an invisible line that we are tied to allowing us to go only a certain distance, but God's sovereignty surpasses the end of that rope. As mentioned earlier in the case of Joseph, his brothers' wicked and seemingly successful plan to sell him appeared to defeat God's will of elevating him. Strangely the wicked plot of Joseph's brothers ended up being the very means by which God accomplished His perfect will in Joseph's life. Joseph's father had made him a coat of many colors, but God Almighty had given Him another coat that was tailored from the warehouse of Heaven and nothing could steal that coat! Nothing is different with you.

Many men and women throughout all of time and history have fought against the truth of God. Yet, in spite of themselves, God has used them as instruments to spread that very truth by calling attention to it and its powers. Just as in the early church Christians were scattered abroad by persecution. So, what happened to them? They ran and as they ran the gospel ran with them. The storm that shakes the trees only aids to scatter the seeds of God in every direction.

History bears out God's sovereignty and His providence!

Rome lasted five hundred years. God used their roads to take the gospel to the known world. Rome was responsible for burning Jerusalem down and yet, who won? God won. That's the sovereignty of God and His providence working together!

DIRECT COMMAND. DIRECT OBEDIENCE.

Nothing is really small with God. He hangs the most momentous weights on the smallest wires. The person who is saved by grace has the advantage of grace. The household of faith has the upper hand. How? Well, all things are not good, but they work together for our good. The root word of providence is the word *provide*. **God provides!** The person who is saved has an extra card in their deck. God's favor comes into our life when we walk in obedience to Him. He places the biggest blessings behind the most ordinary doors. God puts big doors on little hinges.

It would be great if God just showed us every single door for our lives and they magically opened. Now, that wouldn't require much faith. On the contrary, God will orchestrate a situation and place the answer to our prayers in the humblest box. It's up to us to discern this and open the box. God doesn't give explanations, but rather commands. This culture has taught us a strange hesitation and resistance to the voice of God. God gives us a command and what happens? We filter it! We filter out the parts we just don't want to hear. If it doesn't line up with our personality, schedules, or bank accounts we simply disregard it.

God speaks to us and it goes into our mind and our worldly mindset begins to filter it into a cubicle inside of our soul. We are trained by this culture to deflect and resist biblical change. We either think the problem is something unrelated to us or someone else. So, we put God's voice into a box and lay it to the side. The goal of the Holy Spirit is to give us direct instructions and receive direct obedience. Learn to submit to God and not strive with Him. Ask the Holy Spirit to show you how to surrender. What will happen is that God will show you what doors to walk through and what moves to make.

DREAM BOARDS

Brain storming, leadership planning, business management, etc. call them whatever you want. The idea of planning is here to stay. We Pinterest, research, and Google ways to stack our shoes, file our tax documents, and even a better way to unroll toilet tissue. Whatever the case might be, I have some of that "planning board method and mentality" in my madness. Throughout the years, as I have studied or spent time in prayer, I would write things down and stick them on an old corkboard.

A vision that is hard to run with is one that no one ever wrote down. This corkboard is full of thoughts, phrases, sayings, patterns, and principles. If and when God speaks to me, I always try to write down what He is telling me. It may not make any sense to me at the moment, but I know that, in time, I will understand. It never fails.

The moment you got saved, God gave you something that you didn't have before. He gave you sight. You can see! Yet, sight doesn't create anything. It only records what is already existing. The new birth you have in Jesus Christ brings you sight. God gives you new eyes and you can never see things the same. Then you begin to see the bulletin board of your life and all the stuff that is attached to it. You realize that your thinking, talking, walking, and your life concepts have been so disoriented, lost, and backwards. You realize what a fool you were. Your life now has new meaning and you begin to see what God really wanted to place on the dream board of your heart.

As I study, I look at my cork board of thoughts for whatever season that I am in. To anyone else, all these sticky notes and papers wouldn't make a bit of sense. However, to me, I can understand exactly what the common denominator is. All of these seemingly unrelated pages make sense to me. It's the same way in your spiritual development. You now look at your life as a blank bulletin board and God begins to show you the very ingredients that He has for your life.

Every past hurt, pain, and tragedy of your life is written upon the bulletin board inside of your inner man. Jesus Himself said, "Except a man be born again, he cannot see the kingdom of God." Salvation in Christ changes things! It turns the lights on in your life and you see clearly. You enter a dimension that already existed, and you walk into this magnificent reality of the kingdom and you SEE what's already there.

Now, sight doesn't create anything. It only records what already exists. Now you see into a whole new realm. You see how foolish you once were. Your thinking, walking, talking, and life in general have been in the dark. Now you see the true light of

God and you also begin to see something else-YOUR BLUEPRINT!

After Jesus comes in to your life, all of the items on the bulletin board of your life make sense. God now turns your eyes upon what He originally had planned for you upon your conception. The links of the chain of your life now begin to become clear. Through God's providence they are going to start to link up and line up.

The greatest songs, art pieces, and historical treasures all have one thing in common. They were forged over time. For example, a hit song may take only twenty minutes to write, but it usually requires twenty years to live. The song lyrics may have come to life in only minutes, but they were planted long ago. The present moment was just when germination occurred. Amazing Grace wasn't written in the heat of the moment. John Newton wrote the song fifteen years after his personal transformation and salvation. What makes grace so amazing in our life is when it has grown over the years. Grace only grows as you give it out and as you receive it! We don't find gold laying on the sidewalk, but rather buried deep in the ground. You have to dig to find treasure.

Maybe you have an idea that God has shown you which could be the solution to a problem. The Holy Ghost conceives the idea. He then plants the idea in your heart and begins to water it through circumstances, trials, and the encouragement of others.

Write down your vision. Why?

Chaos can become creation the moment God touches it!

THE BOLDPRINT

> **DON'T STRIVE WITH GOD.**
> **SURRENDER TO HIM.**

CHAPTER 14
GREAT MINDS THINK UNLIKE

As kids, we used to put toy soldiers in a row and lead them in a Saturday morning adventure to go fight with other soldiers or whatever figurines were handy. We would line up the soldiers facing against the other and go into a land called make believe.

We, as people, make our plans and place into a perfect order the toy soldiers of our life. These toy soldiers are things such as money, vocation, family, and even the controlling of others. Then God comes and rearranges the order of our soldiers. He moves and shifts things around so that we come to points of discomfort. There wouldn't be any real change unless God rearranged our plans, schemes, and schedules.

We can do the proposing, but God will do the disposing. God crosses up our purposes and often breaks our schedules for great purpose-His purpose.

God in His sovereignty prevails. God in His providence protects. We often don't see God protecting and shifting things around as a good thing. We often think God is hiding something from us. God may be hiding something *for* you, not *from* you. If not for the providence of God, chaos would reign.

God formed mankind and gave him the ability to make choices. Man proposes and has freedom of thought, will power, and free agency. Yet, God has the power to move the soldiers of our life around to garner our attention. What is God after inside of our heart when He reaches for our attention? He wants our worship! If He gets our true worship, then we will get His true blessing. This blessing isn't just confined to money, but on the contrary it covers the entire constitution of man-spirit, soul, and body.

The remarkable thing about providence is that most of the time it is happening, and we aren't fully aware of it. Creativity isn't born in the mundane routine of doing things our way. We don't perform our best when all things are in our control. God moves and shifts things in our life to bring full glory to Himself. The greatest stories of redemption and success seem to rise from the dirt of what appears to be situations that are dark, bleak, and hopeless. Creativity is born in the unfamiliar spaces of life. If you want to find creativity, embrace what seems to require raw faith, hard work, and deep worship. You'll get creative fast!

THE OIL OF CREATIVITY

I've often wondered what makes people creative? How do some people come up with ideas, inventions, and pioneer life-changing works that make us applaud for generations to come? I didn't know when I was a child that God would use the diversity of my childhood tragedies and let-downs to make me what He wanted me to be. I didn't know that growing up in hardship, pain, and neglect would cause my soul to broaden and actually equip me to be able to reach every type of person for Christ.

The anointing of God teaches you to shift and flow with the Holy Spirit. You don't learn this in college and no man can teach this, it must be walked out over time. In order to truly minister to people, you have to become all things to all men. This doesn't mean that you are not being yourself. The anointing of God is typified in the Bible as oil. When your setting and circumstances change, God will give you the oil required for that particular situation.

Let's say that you are not really a kid-type of person. Let's even say that you get frustrated with kids easily. Then, your church asks you to help out with this year's Vacation Bible School. Suddenly, they give you a group of little ones and you feel overwhelmed. However, you realize that God put you in this position and He has anointed you for this task. You excel to the point that parents and others are blown away by your ability to work with kids.

Who knew?

When we are willing to be an open vessel, God is willing to give us the creativity of His oil to flow in whatever situation comes our way!

This doesn't make you fake, it makes you favored! Creativity is, in one sense, the ability from God to function effectively and fruitfully in your gift set (or not) in any circumstance.

WHO IS CREATIVE?

One mistake we make, in terms of creativity, is to think that being creative is limited to one type of person or one type of thinking. We assume that it is a single adverb, adjective, or noun. Creativity isn't confined to just one thought pattern or one type of person. **I believe that creativity is a series of distinct spiritual processes all converging in one season for a divine purpose!**

Creativity can come, emerge, and blossom through the most ordinary person. It is for those who want to create. God sees your life as a solution to a problem. You were NOT born a problem. You were born a sinner, but by the grace of God, you can become the creative, redeemed child of God. This makes you a problem solver!

Creativity isn't reserved only for those who naturally walk in the room and seem to have the creative magic to move people from the wilderness to the promise land. Creativity is for anyone who can get out of bed and try. Then, most importantly, creativity will find those who try again. Creativity finds the person who is not willing to settle for a piece of the pie. They believe that they can have the entire pie, if God baked the pie! People who push through the mud of life are people that find solutions.

We live in a world permeated with *answers*. You can buy an oil, cream, or a pill that seems to be the cure for any present problem. As you know, most people have the answer! Having an answer to a problem is a wonderful thing but requires little to no faith. People seem to have the answer for everything, and most of them will post your answer for you on social media. Having the answer doesn't demand a real change.

Solutions are completely different! Solutions require more than answers. Solutions require faith, process, time, and most likely, **creativity!** Time, for example, will often bring about a space for you to get creative about what God is doing in your life. Getting creative is better than starving. People get into a destiny disease of "one of these days" mentality. They allow time to drift away and they haven't put forth the faith effort to allow God to do a creative work through them.

In order for creativity to come forth, you will have to be pushed out of your safe zone. Comfort zones are not in the Bible and are complete heresy spoken by the Christians of our day. I can promise you that creativity finds the person who is willing to rise and try and to continue to try! The more intense the heat of your fiery trial is, the more creative you will become! The people who are willing to keep trying will ultimately find themselves running into God solutions. That's where creativity comes from.

Creativity isn't all about money. Money is great, but it can rest on your life and it can also fly away from your life. Creativity isn't about the world's definition of success. Anyone can get in front of a camera, act foolish, and if enough people push the foolishness, then suddenly it's a viral sensation. In our culture, sadly, that is what success is. Creativity is about God's will, His Kingdom, and His expression in the earth.

GOD CREATED

Creativity is not a secular idea and is not tied to the arts only. Creator God is the original artist! The Father of lights sprang this entire cosmos into perfect order. The arts, music, and human expression were redeemed through the blood of Christ! Every expression of art, music, and design is either giving God glory or it sprang from a God-given idea, talent, or gift. Yes, I do believe the devil can energize, with demonic passion, artists, entertainers, and suddenly their influence becomes poison that millions drink. However, the God of the Bible is the one who gives gifts unto men. He is the grand architect and creator above all!

The devil steals the heart of people who are gifted. With that thievery he is able to destroy countless souls through deadly influence. Once he steals their heart, their talent, gifting, and creativity are used as his pawn. The end result is death. Look at the great artists of our time. Elvis Presley, Michael Jackson, James Brown, Prince-all talented people who gave their heart to the god of this world. How did that turn out for them? They all died early, and their creativity died with them.

From the onset of time, God has spoken creativity into the heart of man. The earth was without form and void, and darkness covered the face of the entire earth. So, what did God do? He spoke! When He spoke, creation marched from chaos into divine order.

"In the beginning God created...." **Genesis 1:1 (a), King James Version**

The first working of God in relation to this earth was to create. *Creativity comes from the divine mind of God.*

God has even given wicked men ideas that have brought about great blessings for us all. No one is asking where Willis Carrier went to church. They are just thankful for his invention called the air conditioning unit.

Our mistake is that we categorize creativity as one thing. It's not. Creativity is when the separate sparks come together to produce a fire. The fire melts the metal so that it can be shaped into a vessel for use. You don't have to be a neuroscientist to be creative. The Spirit of God is the grand guide in our lives.

I once heard a story of a large movie making studio that was in the process of being built. So, the blueprints were drawn up and the engineers went to work. They designed three separate buildings: a computer science building, the animation building, and a third building for everyone else. A guy by the name of Steve Jobs spoke up and decried the idea. He believed that in order for a product to emerge that could change the world, people from different cultures would need to work together and collaborate. He insisted they design the studio as one large open space. He believed that there needed to be a mixture in order for creativity to emerge. He was right. (Lehrer, 2012).

CONNECTING THE CREATIVE SPARKS

I have been through trials in my life that, at the time, seemed to be an isolated storm. Times have come where I couldn't really reconcile one particular trial and its connectivity to the next one. In the moment it was just the *present fire of life*.

Yet, nothing in God is disconnected from His plan. Every storm is connected to the next one. Somehow and some way, God has so designed it this way. Every trial of your life is systematically connected to the next one. You will harness your spiritual development unless you see this fact. There have been seasons of life that I have been through where I couldn't discern the big realities that God was trying to get into my view. Yet, over time,

I can and have looked back at every fiery season and seen that the flames were connected. God was molding me, not through just one fire, but several fires were converging to bring about change inside of me!

We tend to stay isolated in our little world. God won't have any of that! We normally won't come out of our shell through our own free will. God uses crisis to force us out of the rut of life. God will place us in storms that create friction in our life. It's the friction that creates the spark. The spark produces the fire. The fire warms the room!

HITTING THE WALL

Everyone has seeds of creativity inside of them. When I read I Corinthians 12, I am naturally drawn to the Apostle Paul's teaching on the body of Christ. He teaches us that the body of Christ is likened unto the human body. Of all the metaphors that Paul could have chosen to reveal God's plan in the Earth, he chose the human body. Like a giant puzzle, every child of God who has placed their faith in Jesus fits into this body. When we worship Jesus together, we are worshipping our mutual King. We don't have to lose our unity in diversity. God's body is one coat, but many colors. When Jesus is glorified, the gifts of the Spirit flow, unity is evident, and creativity springs up like a fresh fountain! We don't all worship the exact same way in terms of style. Great minds think *unlike* within the bonds of peace!

I have preached in settings where they had no instruments. I have ministered in places where they had an orchestra and an abundance of singers, minstrels, and talented musicians. True worship isn't about a style. Get creative with your worship and learn to dance with or without a praise team. If you demand a praise team before you truly worship, you've missed the entire point of true praise.

When it comes to fresh creativity in our lives, we all hit the wall in life, business, and family. It's not *if* you will hit the wall, it's *when* you will hit the wall. Whenever you hit the wall in life, simply take what fragments you have and step away for a moment. Often times God will be speaking to me about something in my own life or perhaps giving me a few fragments of something I am supposed to minister. Yet, all I have are those few fragments. What do I do?

Well, I place those fragments in my invisible bag. Sometimes you need to take a long walk to clear the runway of your mind or spirit. I'm not talking about new age meditation, but rather you need to walk away from the wall and get into the secret place. That place may be a walk down the road or inside of a prayer closet. At any rate, God will begin to give you what you are seeking, when you stop seeking IT and you start seeking HIM. Then, the wall won't matter because in Jesus you'll find the door. He's the door through the wall!

JUST DO IT

I once heard a story about the sports empire, Nike, in its early days. The story goes that Nike was in the process of coming up with a slogan for their young company. They worked and worked hard to come up with several ideas and nothing seemed to click. Late one night, someone mentioned the name Gary Gilmore and his story.

Gary Gilmore had murdered a gas station employee and a motel manager in Utah in 1976. On the morning of January 17, 1977, Gilmore was executed. He was asked if he had any last words. While waiting on the firing squad to end his life Gilmore yelled out "Let's do it!" Mind you, Gilmore did not flinch as he was executed.

Nike rejected the new slogan at first, but soon the morbid phrase was translated into "Just Do It." Suddenly Nike had their winning slogan that would take over the advertising world and reign supreme. "Just Do It" would rise to turn a struggling company into a global multibillion-dollar empire (Bella, 2018). Nike executives thought they had hit the wall with their new push to the top and suddenly creativity landed in their lap! The rest is history.

God began to write this book inside of me eleven years ago. Yet, over the next several years, the creativity seemed to die. A few years ago, God brought the remaining fragments to surface and like fresh bread, the loaves began to rise.

Providence was working in the background for the last decade. Creativity was putting the pieces of the puzzle together and the book you're holding is the result!

In God's timing, both providence and creativity would come together and form a blueprint!

UNDERDOGS

God has allowed you to pass through specific circumstances that were tailor-made for you. God knows what environment you're going to thrive in and what soil is best for you to grow in. God has brought people into your life and removed others from your life. He also has removed you from their life (we rarely think of it that way). God is using everything that you have been through. He is using your childhood, whether good or bad. He is using the lessons you have learned and are currently learning to bring glory through your life. Grace is working and patience is being developed through it all. If we let patience have its perfect working within us, we won't lack or be weak in our spiritual infrastructure. Trials fortify our spirit and reinforce the strength and life of our roots in God!

I think of the underdogs in life. These people, through diverse setbacks and heartbreak, rise to the top of life. God loves us all but seems to specifically favor the person whom no one would ever believe could rise to the top in life. That's the scriptural pattern. Man looks on the outside, but God measures us from the inside. God takes people who seem to have no chance in life and brings them to the big dance to win it all!

"He lifts the poor from the dust and the needy from the garbage dump. He sets them among princes, placing them in seats of honor. For all the earth is the LORD's, and he has set the world in order." **I Samuel 2:8, New Living Translation**

When this happens, the glory belongs to Him. If you feel like you have been swimming upstream your entire life, don't give up. There will come a day when you are thankful that God made you take the stairs of life and not the easy, elevator way! Jesus Christ holds the keys to your life. He's going to raise you up from the dust and use you! I bet this is already happening and you're not even aware of it.

THE BOLDPRINT

> ### CONGRATS, YOU'RE THE UNDERDOG.

CHAPTER 15
THE SOIL OF THE SOUL

God is at work in every area of your life. One meeting or divine circumstance can change your life. There are so many people today who hold great positions very different than those they held in earlier days. Some are preaching the gospel of Jesus who once set out for other fields. Others are in other vocational areas and still, in so many ways, they are preaching the gospel.

The farmer is growing a crop to feed the hungry.
The lawyer is defending the defenseless.
The doctor is bringing paths of healing to the sick.

Even with mankind in rebellion, God is still using them to feed His sheep. I have seen God guide men who were lost and undone to Himself through His great providence. If God, in His mercy, guides the affairs of wicked men to lead them unto Himself, then how much more does providence work for those who are His children. The root of providence is the word *provide*. God is **providing** for you!

If you take a comprehensive view of your life, undeniably you'll see God's providence at work. God puts us in the right places at the right time. In the moment, it may seem like it is just the opposite. I can assure you that every time God slammed a door in my face, that it was for my good and His glory.

DON'T BECOME WHAT YOU GO THROUGH

I wonder what is happening under the surface of your life right now; what streams are merging together to bring you to an encounter with God? We often forget that no event happens by chance, but everything, for the child of God, is working for His greater good in all of us.

Strange events may have led you into the occupational field you are in now. Providence is the doorway that is designed to lead us to our destiny. If providence is the door, then choices are the doorknob. God ultimately picks the hallways, doorways, and the timing to which we will walk through them. We may throw the dice, but God determines how they fall! This led to that and that led to this, then here you are! You may be in a sobering season where you feel like you have missed the mark in certain areas of your life.

Whatever your current season is in life, I want you to consider something. Every single thing that has happened to you has played a role in making you the person you are right now. God, by His grace, will not allow any situation to be wasted in your life!

How does someone become bitter? They go through bitter things and those bitter things go through them. They become what they go through.

How does someone become joyful? They go through similar pain in life, but somehow, they keep their focus clear on the greater good. It may sound like heresy, or it may sound too simple, but it's true: everything you are has come as a result of what you have been through as well as your response to what you've been through.

Never get addicted to the sweetness of the good season.
Never get addicted to the poison of the bad season.

Every season has, within its duration, an invitation and opportunity for us to internally give up. The reasons will always seem legitimate, but they are not of God. Be committed to what God is going to do up the road, and not to what the enemy has already done. Our natural tendency is to simply give up! Don't do it!

I look back on my life and I think to myself "Well, this was terrible, or that was good, but everything that happened brought something of value to my life." What happens when we walk through dark times is that we tend to let the darkness settle too long. I'm not even suggesting we should just always be on top of the mountain with a smile on our face. I'm saying that we need to rent trials, not own them. That darkness will become cement if we aren't careful!

Every valley in life brings a soil for your soul that God uses to create roots. What's His purpose for this? Fruit. God will bring a glorious fruit from every single dark place of your life. Don't rush God, He lays sure foundations. He will put all the fragments together in the right season!

Life is a coagulation of seasons. Just like in the natural, there are the seasons of winter, spring, summer, and fall; so it is with the spiritual journey. There are seasons where things are just pleasant, secure, and as peachy as a spring morning. Then there are dying seasons where the winter of life has chilled our hearts to the bone. This is normal!

A BUMP ON YOUR HEAD

People want to be told "Everything is going to be alright." Now, according to the Word of God, we know that man looks on the exterior of things and makes his judgment, but God examines what's happening on the inside. We want to eat what we want, drink what we want, and live how we want, then ask a doctor to give us a pill to undo all these decisions. This is a stain on our culture. Now, to the child of God who has placed his or her faith in Christ, they have a lawyer named Jesus in every litigation of their life. However, to the person who has rejected God and decided that they would live their own way, he or she has no advocate.

I've met with people who have gone through seasons of rebellion or made horrible decisions and I know what they want me to say, "It's going to be okay."

Sometimes, it's not going to be okay. Sometimes, we have to go to bed with a bump on our head. That's not deep spirituality, that's usually the normal results of disobedience. Sin brings a sad harvest. If you think obedience to God is hard, try rebellion against God.

If you are in the mud of messed up living, here's your hope. God sees where you are. God loves you. God isn't thrilled about where you are. However, the road out of the mess has a sign far off in the distance that reads "grace and mercy...this way!"

The moment we surrender to God is the moment that we can claim God's grace as it extends to us in our despair. Grace will lead you out of this garden of weeds. Grace and mercy serve as weed removal tools in our mess. Grace and mercy are God's garden tools to uproot what we have planted, or allowed to be planted. The road to recovery may not be short-lived, but grace and mercy will absolutely make the ride smoother. You'll have a peace that "everything is going to be alright" even as it seems to be just the opposite.

THE MAN IN THE MIDDLE

The fine print of your life has been leading you to someone. His name is Jesus Christ. Controversy surrounds His very name and for good reason. Demons fear His name, His power, and His Lordship. Politicians fear Him lest they lose a vote. To declare His name is to declare His Word and what He has said to us. God the Father didn't stop talking when Jesus went back to Heaven! The Holy Spirit still speaks today concerning Jesus Christ, the Divine One. The One to whom every knee must bow!

We all must meet up with Him at some point. At some turn of the road, we are confronted by His lordship. It's here that we accept the King, or we decide we will form our own kingdom. The only trouble is that the King has our paperwork (blueprint). To the person reading this who has already given their life to Christ, you know the moment that this happened. Christ makes sense of the madness of this life.

My life began to take shape when I got saved. I began to see that what and who God wanted me to be was irreplaceable. Getting to know Jesus is the key to unlocking the blueprint for our lives. Our life doesn't have to be a wobbly way where we trip, stumble, and crawl into our destiny. Trust me, there will be enough struggle along the way. Destiny and purpose are to be discovered here while on Earth. Our time here on Earth is a dressing room for eternity. We are to occupy until Jesus comes, and our assignment is to find our assignment! Sovereignty is the fact that God already knows and is ever in control, all the while, He aims all humanity toward Heaven through His Son, even as billions reject Him and perish. In between decision and sovereignty stands a man-<u>Jesus Christ!</u>

God provided (root word of providence) a lamb for a house, a lamb for a nation, and a lamb for the entire world! God delivered up His Son to die. In the fullness of time, God knew the links of the chain of His plan would line up. So, is life based on our decisions or God's sovereignty? **The answer is both.**

Standing in the middle of religion of man and relationship with God was a man-Jesus Christ.

The ideology that we are all children of God is false. Now, we are all God's creation, but not everyone has been redeemed! We ARE all children of Adam and Eve, but to say there are many ways to Heaven is simply false. The entire doctrine of destiny that comes from media, famous lips, or celebrities is bogus. These shallow theologies are built on the bologna that life is just one big maze and a higher power is perhaps guiding all people to the same harbor.

Divine providence DOES NOT come from the power within, but rather from above. Following your heart is NOT the plan of

God. God created your heart. Give your heart to Him and He will sanctify your desires and make them His desires. He will scrape the taste buds of your life clean and give you a new hunger for Him. You telling God how to navigate the labyrinth of your life, is like you telling Henry Ford how to fix his truck.

A WOMAN'S RIGHT

In the most improbable way, and at the time least expected, God will meet up with us. A person who has silenced the voice of God for years may suddenly see a truth that they ignored a thousand times. Suddenly, in the providence of God, truth strikes their core and their heart bursts open, the mind clears up, and the scales fall off. This is called salvation!

Case in point is a story found in John 4. Jesus left Judea and headed for Galilee. This is about a sixty to seventy-mile journey. Sitting directly in the middle of Judea and Galilee was ancient Samaria.

"Jesus *__had to go__* through Samaria." **John 4:4, God's Word Translation**

There is one reason above all that Jesus had to go through this town. The reason was for us to have this story. This account was given to us because of divine providence. It is an account of providence at work in real time!

He came to a well there called Jacob's well. Jacob's well is not

172

mentioned in the Old Testament. What is mentioned is a plot of ground that Jacob had purchased where he pitched his tents after his reconciliation with his brother, Esau. He purchased the land for a hundred pieces of money and built an altar there. This well was perhaps dug by Jacob and was on or near this land that he purchased. Remember his father Isaac, and grandfather had dug wells throughout their journey as aliens in a foreign land. Abraham had come into the land of Canaan as an outsider and his son Isaac was considered the same by the Philistines. In fact, Isaac had to re-dig the wells that Abraham had dug. They had been stopped up.

Jacob bought a piece of land. Upon his death, he would be buried here.

Jacob's children would go into slavery but would be rescued through the providence of God via Joseph and Moses. Before the children of Jacob left Egypt, they would bring the dead bones of Joseph out of Egypt and bury them in the plot of ground his father Jacob had purchased. What a story!

Joseph had lived in Egypt for most of his life. He had given his people a direct order that when God delivered them from bondage, to take his bones with them. When the day came, Moses fulfilled this order.

The nation of Israel came out of Egypt accompanied by a coffin. The bones of Joseph were taken and buried in the plot of ground that Jacob his father had purchased near Sychar. *This is the place that Jesus had to go through.*

In Bible days, the father's blessing was a thing to be strongly desired and attained. Jacob, the son of Isaac, the son of Abraham, had pulled his entire family together and told them of things to come. He prophetically gave each of his children blessings and admonitions for the future. He looked at his son Joseph and said the following:

"Joseph is a fruitful bough (vine) by a well: whose branches run over the wall." **(Genesis 49:22, King James Version).**

Jacob saw his Joseph as a spiritual vine planted by a well. He knew that all the forces of darkness would come against Joseph, but that God Almighty would be his help.

There, in this geographical region, are the bones of Joseph.

There, in this geographical region, is the well of Jacob.

There, in this geographical region, was the providence of God.

Jesus went through this region to give us a living picture of how providence works.

There at noon, he met a woman of Samaria at the well. He asked her for a drink. She was puzzled as to why a Jew would ask a Samaritan for a drink. Jews had no dealings with Samaritans and considered them to be less than themselves. If she only knew who it was that was sitting at the well with her!

Jesus explained to her that there were two types of water in this life. One was temporary water and one was eternal! She asked him for this eternal water.

"Go and get your husband," Jesus told her. **John 4:16, New Living Translation**

Suddenly, her life unraveled and unfolded before her eyes.

"I don't have a husband," the woman replied. Jesus said, "You're right! You don't have a husband— for you have had five husbands, and you aren't even married to the man you're living with now. You certainly spoke the truth!" **John 4:17-18, New Living Translation**

He read her spiritual mail and she ran into the city to proclaim "Come, see a man, which told me all things that I ever did, is not this the Christ?" There, at Jacobs well, the vine of Joseph (Jacob's son of favor) was still blooming. There at noon, her life changed forever. Providence is not limited to time. Thousands of years after Jacob died, the well he dug was still a place of divine providence.

Who has stood in the road of providence in your life? Perhaps what you thought was an inconvenient detour led you to the blueprint God had for you.

THE BOLDPRINT

THE FINE PRINT OF YOUR LIFE IS
LEADING YOU TOWARD SOMEONE.
HIS NAME IS JESUS.

CHAPTER 16
BIG DOORS LITTLE HINGES

The world is caught in a fog. Blind to sin, and if that's not bad enough, completely aloof to our surroundings. Our attention and our focus are the prizes being fought over. Drive a car and you will see people attempting to multi-task behind the steering wheel! We are at war to maintain our focus. Often times, providence comes our way and we, of course, are in a fuzzy cloud of day-to-day living. Technology has almost made us entirely detached from the present reality of our life. It is called fantasy for a reason!

In reality, if you look around you can see a distinct foggy vibe that people are caught in. Here's what is sad: all moments aren't created equal. We are missing moments with family to check an unimportant text message. The woman at the well in John 4 was talking to the very Son of God and was completely unaware of the moment she was caught up in. God shows up in big ways that are capsuled in small moments or circumstances. I wish I could tell you how many times I have counseled people that I've wanted to say, "The answer you are looking for is right under your nose." Rarely, is the solution to our problem far off in the foggy distance. Normally, it is simply a spiritual problem we need to address. Circumstances may not change, but I can change my perspective of them. That's the power of prayer, it changes us.

RUNNING IN CIRCLES

Long before Jacob dug a well of generational life, his past was quite eventful. His birth was a unique circumstance! His mother Rebekah was barren and couldn't have children. Miraculously, she conceived. Jacob and his twin brother, Esau, jostled in the womb of their mother, Rebekah.

This would be a lasting omen of their lives. Because of parental partiality, there came a division in their home. Rebekah favored Jacob, and Isaac, their father, favored Esau. Through a conspiracy, Jacob stole the birthright and blessing from his brother, Esau. His old blind father was ready to release the fatherly blessing upon his sons and Jacob placed goat hair upon his body to play the part of his brother. Blind Isaac had no idea that he was blessing Jacob with Esau's blessing.

Esau became enraged and vowed to kill his brother for the shenanigan.

The only option for young Jacob was to run away from home.

Yet, anytime you are running from God, you are running in circles.

"Meanwhile, Jacob left Beersheba and traveled toward Haran. At sundown he arrived at a good place to set up camp and stopped there for the night. Jacob found a stone to rest his head against and lay down to sleep. As he slept, he dreamed of a stairway that reached from the earth up to heaven. And he saw the angels of God going up and down the stairway. At the top of the stairway stood the LORD, and he said, 'I am the LORD, the God of your grandfather Abraham, and the God of your father, Isaac. The ground you are lying on belongs to you. I am giving it to you and your descendants.'" **Genesis 28:10-13, New Living Translation**

It wouldn't take long before Jacob was weary from running. I can tell you firsthand that even in the will of God, you will get weak, tired, and run out of gas. However, when you are out of God's will there is an all-consuming exhaustion that you can't seem to shake off.

Sin pushes us out of the place God wants us to be. It doesn't mean that God abandons us, but He simply withdraws and allows us to run on our power until the power source runs out. The only thing left for us is death or deliverance. Jacob is about to come out of the fog he's been living in.

THE MIDDLE OF NOWHERE

In the middle of nowhere, Jacob stops. **Genesis 28:11(a), King James Version** says, "he lighted upon a ***certain place…***". God has allowed him to run, but Jacob is out gas, time, and energy. He's about to have an encounter with God that he will never forget. He's tired…and mostly tired of himself! He thinks he's in a safe place. No one will bother him here at this rest stop. Jacob thinks he is alone, but alone he isn't.

God will show up in the places and moments where no one else in the known universe could find you. God can find you in places that the devil himself won't go! God will find you at the lowest of low or the highest of highs. This "certain" place is where God stops us in our tracks and forces us to confront something in our life-whether good or bad! Often God will slow us down to cause our gratitude to rise. Other times, God will slow us down to reveal something dangerous in our life that could potentially destroy us. Both situations are a merciful blessing from God. If you feel like you're in the middle of nowhere, *have hope!*

The sun was setting, and Jacob took a rock or pillar and used it as a pillow. He drifted off to sleep and entered another world.

STAIRWAY FROM HEAVEN

Jacob's dream was unbelievable. In his dream, a ladder or stairway, fell from Heaven to Earth with angels running up and down. The Lord stood at the top of it speaking directly to Jacob.

God has a way of getting our attention. He will get our attention even if it requires a major inconvenience. Save your time and give God your undivided attention.

Our society knows all about ladders. Untold millions rise up every day in hopes of climbing social ladders of money, success, business, etc. The only ladder that matters is the one that Jesus Christ, Himself, is standing atop. If God isn't in the plans, you don't want them. Stop trying to climb some invisible ladder of man and start chasing God. He will drop His ladder over your life. So, what happens then?

You'll have the strength to climb it.
You won't slip and fall into destruction.
You won't have to step on others through envy, malice, or competition.

God has tailor-made His blueprint for you! His pen has designed a pattern and plan for you, and you alone.

Moses had one burning bush.
David had one notable giant.

Joseph had one coat of many colors.
Jacob had one ladder from Heaven.

God has one will for you. He doesn't have multiple options in case this or that doesn't work out. Notice, at the top of the ladder in Jacob's dream stood the Lord. God's direction for our life is always upward and onward! If you are running from God, *STOP!*

I don't want you to stop and give me all the answers to life. I just want you to stop running. You can't turn around until you stop running around in circles. God is dropping a ladder from Heaven upon you today; *it's a book and you are reading it now.* Your wakeup call has come, so answer the call!

The Lord spoke to Jacob and informed him that He knew his father Isaac and He knew His grandfather Abraham. The land he was sleeping on was a part of God's plan for him and his children.

PILLARS AND PILLOWS

When Jacob woke up, he was rattled by the experience.

"When Jacob woke up, he thought 'Surely the LORD is in this place, and I was unaware of it.' And he was afraid and said, 'How awesome is this place! This is none other than the house of God; this is the gate of heaven!'" **Genesis 28: 16-17, Berean Study Bible**

To have God knocking on the door of your life, and not know it, is a scary place to be. If this is your case, it doesn't have to remain this way. If God is knocking on your heart, open the door and let Him in.

Jacob took the rock of earth that he had used for a pillow and poured oil on the top of it. This demonstrates the significance of this moment in his life. It wasn't just another day for him, and it doesn't have to be for you either. Jacob turned his pillow (a place where he would have stopped and perhaps let life just pass him by) into a holy place. He hit rock bottom and found that the rock at the bottom is where God does His best work.

The place of breakdown can also be the place of breakthrough if you'll receive the ladder of Heaven. Don't let it take falling off that ladder for you to look up to God as Creator, Father, and the Almighty! Jacob called the name of the place, Bethel. Bethel means *House of God*. The place had formally been called "Luz," which means almond. Sound crazy?

Well, an almond is a little thing, but with God, big doors swing on little hinges. The Lord turned a small spot in the road into a place where Jacob was shaken by the power of God. With God, nothing is really small. He hangs the finest blueprints on the smallest wires. God will hide the blessings, not from us, but for us!

What's the problem? It just seems far too simple for us. Well, how hard do you want to make this? Don't miss the biggest blessings of God because you couldn't recognize a small door.

MOMENTS

I often hear people say things like "One of these days, I'm going to do such and such."

Our culture is baited with distractions that lead us to a dangerous procrastination. I'm not talking about simple things like not taking out the trash. I'm talking about the reality that we are in a war for our focus.

We think within ourselves that if we can get to a certain place that we will be able to accomplish this, or that thing, that we have put off for some time. One of the little lies of the devil is "one of these days."

It is a lie that there's this mystical place up the road in life where all these situations won't exist as they do now. That's just life.

I have come to a sobering truth. If I don't create memories with my children, family, and those who are most important to me, then time will evaporate before my eyes and I will miss precious moments ordained by God. My children will soon be in another town. My family will be constantly changing. People will be coming into my life and others will be going out of my life.

We come to terms with our physical bodies. If we don't properly take care of them, we usually increase our chances of bodily breakdown. Time shows us that we are mortal. I have found out that if I decide I'm going to pray tomorrow, that the enemy will bring about something to detour that prayer time before the sun rises.

I must recognize that life is happening right before my eyes. The curtain to this life has been lifted and the scenes of this life are unfolding.

There is no happy place in the distant future that just falls on our head by accident. I have bought the lie before that…

If I ever get these bills paid off…
If I ever get this project at Creative Church done…
If I ever get this healthy…
If I ever get this base or that base covered…

Some may say "One of these days, I'll be where I want to be." Well, I guess if you have an accidental goal then this may be a true statement. However, if you want to be at peace as you look back over the shoulder of your life, then, by all means, don't miss God-ordained moments. They may seem small and fragile, but in actuality, they are big and precious.

I used to believe that if I could get to some apex point in my life and stand on some invisible mountain with my hands lifted up, then that would be the pinnacle of life. That usually doesn't happen in the way we are imagining it will.

While we are planning, preparing, and purposing what we will do, life is happening right under our nose. I don't believe God designed for us to hit one apex of the journey and be satisfied with that. For me, it's the little moments that are the biggest deals in life... moments that we take for granted with people that care the most about us. Why do we place these people out of arms reach of utmost attention, love, and fellowship? Simply put, we think we can take care of that stuff later. Later may never come.

DRINKING FROM MUD PUDDLES

Mission trips are now more similar to vacations than ever before. Nowadays, you can raise some funds and go to a faraway place and call it missions. Yes, I realize that a person doesn't have to starve to death to go on a real mission's trip and the term is very broad.

The bigger point is something happens when we view the conditions and personal economy of others. Our hearts are torn, and we come to the reality of how life is for others. Often, we see ourselves as the blessed ones, but, just as often, we see their hope, joy, and peace and it rattles our theology. When we go somewhere where kids are drinking from a mud puddle, and the level of living is so far below our own, it does something distinct in our hearts.

The separation from our normal life is usually where the change starts. We are out of our environment of routine and comfort. Life somewhere else is offering us a dose of perspective and usually this is something that we unknowingly need. There are places in the world where people go down to the river to bathe and even run the risk of being robbed, raped, or murdered on the trip. I have known people that do mission work in these areas and they usually come home and struggle for weeks to readapt to the *American way*. I have known missionaries who returned home from areas where children were eating out of a garbage can. Upon their return, they struggled to simply get back to normal.

What we take for granted is considered a luxury in some parts of the world. Now, I realize everyone doesn't come back from a mission trip affected in such a deep way. Yet, it does open our eyes to the perspective of real life. I struggle to complain about my life when I look around and see kids who have no family and no one to adopt them.

YOUTH CAMP ZOMBIES

When I was a kid, I went to Christian summer camps every year. I couldn't wait to get to camp! I lived for it! I could never sleep the night before leaving for camp. It's up early and off you go for an exhilarating week of change. You leave the normal life behind for a week and you go to the unknown land of adolescent zombie land. When you arrive, it's all about feeling things out and getting to know other kids from elsewhere. At first, it's weird but of course by the end of the day you have found a friend or two. You don't sleep much at summer camp, so by the end of the week, you feel like a raspy throat zombie.

Summer camp was great. You laugh, cry, and come to Jesus countless times! Then, comes the challenge of returning home to your old friends, old ways, and old habits. It's tough. You've had this experience with God that has gone all the way into your inner man. You're on fire for Jesus!

Providence is like summer camp-it's rare, yet it's full of monumental moments that change our life. When God invites you on a spiritual journey of transformation, accept the invite. Repentance is a gift from God, just as shame is a gift from the devil. God offers us the free gift that costed Jesus everything. That gift is the gift to start over in life. Ladders from God don't fall from the sky every day. When God offers you a providential sign from Heaven, by all means, take the sign and obey!

What if God was showing you a sign of change, giving you a token of mercy, or offering you a door of providence? Would you even recognize that it was Him?

BLIND IGNORANCE VS. BOLD FACE REBELLION

Life will teach you the difference between an innocent blindness versus a sneaky rebellion. A child often times does not know they are in some type of danger. Many times, they get too close to the ledge of danger and fall off. We, as parents, pick them up and dust them off! That's our job. Raising children will teach you more about God than maybe anything else in this current life. The lesson isn't complete when a child, through mere ignorance, makes a mistake. A child who is very small simply just doesn't know any better. It's our job to stop in the middle of the child's crisis and with the voice of calm and direction, teach the child the better way. Ignorance is simply blindness.

It's not that the child does not want to learn. We, as parents, don't want to see our children injured physical, socially, or mentally. However, often times when a child falls down in life, that's when they truly learn. There is a huge difference between the ignorance of a person who is trying hard but has no true experience in a certain area versus a person who is not willing to try due to some form of quiet, or overt rebellion.

The habits, hurts, and hang ups we incur throughout life seem to come like mold on a shower wall. It starts small and unaddressed. Then, what is not given attention and isn't corrected begins to multiply and the mold becomes visible. Life brings disappointments, troubles, and let downs in every shape and size. Then, when left unaddressed, those heartaches become mold in the soil of our soul. Now that very soil that God wants to plant a garden in becomes hardened, or even worse-unfit (cursed) ground!

When issues are left unchecked, they develop roots inside of us that last for years. We can't allow the mold of let-down to grow.

It usually grows into a root of offense, and then bitterness sets in.

God would meet up with us if we were more aware of His presence. He wants to invade our space, but it's full of hurt. We are like a child who doesn't know that there is a better way and we keep walking in ignorance. People don't perish because of a lack of church, money, or prayer, but rather a lack of knowledge. Furthermore, ignorance is not simply being uneducated... it's just blindness for whatever reason.

TREASURE VERSUS TRASH

Our life education is the ability to perceive an opportunity when it comes and to seize it. We pretend like this is easy to do, but there are unemployed, talented people everywhere. A resilient, reliable, trustworthy, faithful man or woman will get a great job much sooner than a person who is possibly greater in talent but lacks initiative. People are looking for the person who is the opportunist! Perception is the ability to understand, extract, and utilize the elements of a situation for the greater good. The farmer has a plow and seed. The earth has soil and substance. God has sunlight and rain. Together, they bring us the bread of the field!

Real education comes first to the heart before it does the head. A few days ago, I was explaining to my son that milk does not come from the grocery store. He looked puzzled. I explained how the cow gives us milk on the dairy farm. My son asked, "Daddy, don't cows pee too? Why don't we drink that?"

"Yes son, yes they do. God made treasure (milk) and God made trash (urine)." If you can't, or don't, perceive that some things are treasure and other things are trash then you will end up drinking the wrong things in life. The ability to perceive and learn is a lost art. To walk in an awareness of God gives you a discernment in all situations. You will be able to quickly spot what is treasure and what is trash.

I don't want you to live, spiritually, miles away from the blueprint that God has for your life! I don't want you to drink the poison of the American nightmare. A person who can't or will not recognize a big door swinging on one of God's little hinges lives a shadowless life. They may be successful, but they won't leave a shadow of life behind them. You only die once, but you live every day!

Many times, God has brought us to a variety of doors and we simply stand there, turn away, or rebel and end up walking in disobedience. Then what happens is we get dull to these *Jacob's Ladder* type of moments in our life. How many present moments of providence have we missed due to the fact that we missed the last few moments of providence? Whenever we ignore God's will, it gets a little easier the next time to ignore! That's where the danger zone begins! It's hard to get out of that danger zone. You will go from ignorance to rebellion and not even know it happened. Life is costly. If you disagree, then raise children. Life is expensive, but ignorance and rebellion can cost you an arm and a leg. Literally!

SCHOOL COLORS ARE BLACK AND BLUE

There are two schools in this life. One is the School of Wisdom. Wisdom stands and shouts out her lessons to all who will hear and obey. There are layers and grades in the School of Wisdom, and you can never know it all! The School of Wisdom offers warnings unto those who are walking down its hallways.

"Don't do that," shouts wisdom!

The tuition and price of admission to the School of Wisdom is due before and during your term.

For example, the cost of wisdom is discipline. You can be talented, yet undisciplined and you will never go to the next grade in this school. You will fail or retake the lesson when the time comes.

The other school in this life is the School of Consequence. Consequence doesn't shout anything except "enjoy now, pay later." Now, I remind you that it shouts this very soft, subtly, and quickly. Almost like one of those commercials where they are selling something that seems too good to be true. At the end of those commercials, there will come an announcer's voice that will be very subtle, but with lightning quick speed he will give you the actual details of the deal. There is a reason that it sounds too good to be true. It's fantasy. That's why it sounds perfect in the moment.

The costly tuition and astronomical price of admission to the School of Consequence comes due *after* the class is over. Usually the cost of this school is a lost marriage, pain, sorrow, or years of your life. The school colors are black and blue. The bruises from this school mark your soul for a long time.

People have lost years of their life in the School of Consequence. Some are still paying off the tuition.

One of the things that wisdom has taught me is to be all, give all, and get all (real education) that I can from every season that God brings me into. I don't want to look back and see that I took for granted any blessing in my life. I want to perceive, discern, and be fully aware of the people, places, and seasons of God's providence. These things tend to change; therefore, I want to have little to no regret when they are gone.

The old lady you helped out at the grocery store may be an angel sent from God.

The little kid that you were kind to may grow to be an agent of change.

The single mother that you gave a Christmas blessing to may end up owning her own company.

Pay attention to the little moments. God often will draw blueprints right inside the very sandbox of your life. Nothing is small with God. He will attach the biggest blessings to the smallest principles. Don't skip servant class. You will need the experience from servant class as long as you live!

What the world will call a mere coincidence, the Bible calls providence!

In between being and not being is our ability to turn the knob on the door of choice. We make decisions and our decisions make us.

THE BOLDPRINT

> ## "ONE OF THESE DAYS..."
> ## IS A LIE FROM THE DEVIL.

CHAPTER 17
DOWNSTREAM

Let's end this book the way we began. Let's get off the train where we got on it. So, picture yourself down the road of life. Everything you are planting right now you will see come out of the ground in the future. Don't make bad decisions and then pray for crop failure! Everything flows downstream in life, so be careful what you pour when you're upstream.

The hands of providence are watching to see if they can move in your direction or sit folded while you wander through life. I have prayed for people who were on their death bed before and I have never heard any of them say "Time has just dragged by. My life has moved at snail pace."

No one argues about that particular truth. Time seems to be evaporating quicker than ever before! Life is moving and time is ticking. All roads meet at the grave and the question is really "What are you going to do with the time you have left?" Recently, I was counseling a young man and he was torn about what direction to go with college. He said, "I want to go ahead and finish medical school but if I do, I'll be thirty-eight when I'm done with that."

I said, "You're going to be thirty-eight anyway."

He said, "Yeah, true."

Time flies.

You can't start over and relive any moment of your life, but you can start today. There is nothing new under the sun. History simply repeats itself, but yours doesn't have to! You can change your history by changing your future. That decision happens in the present moment. Don't stand at the judgement seat of Christ and be sick to death as you gaze throughout the cinematic reel of your life and see the times God was sending providence.

Don't over analyze where you currently are. Life is meant to be lived first from above! You can't live outwardly until you learn how to live inwardly. I refuse to not live a life worthy of its calling! God called you and He called me. I want to run the race He gave me, and I want that for you.

What derailed you? Tragedy? Pain? Losses? Crosses? Headaches and heartaches?

Whatever happened *has* happened. Let it flow **_downstream._**

LOUD AND CLEAR

You don't have to read Christian books to hear the phrase "God has a plan for you" anymore. Nearly every person who believes in some form of higher power subscribes to this slogan. Sometimes, when someone says that you just want to respond "Really, really He does?" It becomes so used that it quickly becomes the hit song that no one wants to hear anymore. God's blueprint for your life doesn't lose its power through use but rather through abuse.

Hear me loud and clear, **God has a blueprint for your life.** Again, I tell you, **God has a blueprint for you.**

One more time, **God has a tailor-made script with your name on it.**

I am thoroughly convinced that every detail of our lives is continually woven together to fit into God's plan of bringing good into our lives, glory to His name, and the fulfillment of His high-designed purpose!

Christianity has failed us in the area of kingdom vocation. We have sat by and let others teach us about our future. Colleges offer us massive debt to get a degree that doesn't fulfill us. Most people live in a blind bubble in relation to their true destiny. They couldn't give you a true answer about why they are here. They can't give you an ounce of eternal perspective about their life. They are alive, but not truly living, though they think they are.

They don't know why they are here. They can tell you what they do for a living, but they can't tell you the fundamental or spiritual reasons God allowed their existence. Yet, God so distinctly designed, formed, and placed them in this life with blueprints included.

Most people have never found the will of God outside of their initial salvation. Getting saved does not mean you automatically fall into the divine drawings for your life. Getting saved only reveals the overall sketch for the plan that God has for us. Seeking God for the components of your blueprint is another thing, yet a thing worth seeking no doubt!

The model of education in our country is simple. You go to school, you graduate from college, and then life will filter out the ones who don't rise to the top. You get a diploma and usually that's it: off you go into the work field. I have no issue with education models, but I do believe that we tend to follow the green, instead of the dream.

God has a plan for you. Don't minimize it. If others mock it, don't you make the same mistake. Don't despise God's plan though it appears to be small to others.

100 MILLION PEOPLE CAN BE WRONG

Are you happy with the direction you're going and occupation you currently occupy? Whenever someone hates their job, it is a weight that their entire family has to carry. If you are a vegetarian and you are rigid about the vegetarian lifestyle, then you don't need to work for Oscar Meyer Meat Company. If you are rigid about your vegan lifestyle, then you don't eat meat and you don't feel others should either. Your passion won't last very long in a field you are not designed to be in. We are not angry with a fish because he doesn't walk on land or with an elephant if he doesn't swim in the ocean. God's design must be honored.

The standards of happiness seem to be set upon a broken scale. The overwhelming majority of Americans live in decent to modest homes (though it would be considered a mansion to others in poor countries) with a decent salary. Though we have an array of economic statuses, the majority of people operate in the middle class.

Who makes the rules when it comes to the standards of what it means to be happy or successful?

Can one hundred million people be wrong? Well, yes. Yes, they can.

Having things that we seem to enjoy certainly isn't poison, in fact, Jesus taught us to seek first His Kingdom and other things would be added to our life.

"Therefore I say unto you, What things soever ye desire, when ye pray, believe that ye receive them, and ye shall have them."
Mark 11:24, King James Version

The Bible doesn't tell us that it's against the rules to have things. We are not only allowed to have things but encouraged to pray for things. We should pray for our needs and desires. Here's where it gets twisted: God will give you the desires of your heart, but those desires have to be reborn desires.

Our desires are often a hidden hurdle to our spiritual development. We get in **our** own way. Notice the scripture doesn't say "Whatever you desire, believe that you will receive it and you will."

The phrase "when ye pray" is the key. Why? Because in prayer, God will jettison an idea in our heart, or He will dismiss it. That seems a little militaristic, but it's actually the mercy of God saving us from a thousand woes! Taste buds go through life cycles. They tell us that our taste buds are changing, growing, or dying every 10 to 14 days. One way that God changes our taste buds is by allowing us to taste something that we *think* we want. It's like tasting soup that is a little too hot for our taste. Immediately, we jerk our mouth away. Guess what? When that happens, you just killed your taste buds. New ones will grow! God will turn up the heat to reveal the motive behind our motive!

FRAIL FAKE FILTERS

Culture has created the measuring stick for our society. What once was profane is now completely normal. Our society says if you don't have a big home, children who have it all, and all the money to develop the perception that all is well, then you must not be successful. If you popped into the home of the average American family on most evenings, you would find a parent, or parents, working themselves to death to support the financial tab of relevance.

Where did this invisible pressure to maintain a certain lifestyle come from? If given the chance to answer, most would give you the basic answer of "I'm just trying to pay the bills, to survive, and get my kids through school, etc." Those are good answers but they are not the only answers. No one wants to eat well, attain nice things, and have their children dressed well more than I do. However, in our nation kids are bullied for what they wear, eat, hair style, and on and on.

Now, peeking back into that home we just spoke about for a minute, you will see exhaustion in parents, kids in different parts of the house on technology, and a slow death in real relationships taking place. Our society is teaching us to ignore the authenticity in others and purchase the fraud part of other people. Everything in our life is processed, from the chicken we eat to the images we post.

It seems that you aren't really successful unless you maintain a certain image and level of living. God doesn't have a filter we can use to crop out the parts we don't like, agree with, or want to see. God isn't concerned with saving our image, but rather saving our *soul*. The filters that we use to view the lives of others are not real! Again, I say, the filters we use to see the life of someone else through IS NOT the reality of what is going on in that person's life. It's a frail, fake, and altered view of reality.

Real love can't be *just* texted, emailed, or messaged to someone. It needs to be **heard** and **felt**. God's love doesn't filter anything. He loves you and He made the rules on what our lives should look like. When I say, "God loves you" …most likely that hits your mental filter and you sort of put it on a shelf. You may think "How does a God I have never seen have an invisible plan for me that I can't currently see?" The instant access of our times may end up being our undoing. We can get something instantly; however, with God there are no drive thru breakthroughs. We must allow God to remove the filter and give us an authentic reality.

God may wear a suit and tie and He may not. I don't know. I can tell you that in the vocation of ministry, we have a monstrous size problem of image distortion. A quick picture of a person on a stage is our view of a minister. Now, you can hate, love, or be indifferent to any style, size, or group of Christians. You may not care at all. I only use this vocation as an example because I am one.

The devil whispers, "This is what you need to be. This is what you need to look like. This is what the goal of life is."

Lie.

Don't believe that for a second. You may see the Lord show up in the eyes of a single parent raising several kids. Don't try to find God through the filter of someone else's false reality that they are trying to project as being real.

NO ARMS, NO LEGS, NO PROBLEM

I heard a story of a man who came into the world with neither arms nor legs, with no medical explanation. Later, he was diagnosed with tetra-amelia syndrome. It's a rare disorder characterized by the absence of all four limbs. I would bet his parents sat in shock upon his delivery.

What a shock.

Little did they know that one day, this baby boy would be someone who would inspire and motivate untold millions from all walks of life. Later in life, this man traveled the world telling others about his story and his faith in God.

Now, here's a guy with no arms and no legs. What would cause a person like this to rise above his dire circumstance?

A better question is why are people so moved by his story?

They see a guy who is limbless standing with a smile on his face and it shreds every cultural standard of what is considered to be the prerequisites of happiness. This story assaults all we think to be important. It gives us a fresh perspective without any filters.

Let me tell you three words that will kill your future: me, me, and me. Let me tell you three more words that will sabotage your life: I, I, and I.

The devil comes along and shows us another person and says "Look, they have it all together. You should get a divorce and move on." When you see other people that seem to have it all together. Remember in reality, they could be living the perfect nightmare. Comparison is a killer. Life is flowing downstream, so remember to make choices you can swallow later.

THE BOLDPRINT

> ### ARE OTHERS MOCKING YOUR BLUEPRINT? DON'T MAKE THAT SAME MISTAKE.

CHAPTER 18
OPENING THE PACKAGE

It's easier to learn than it is to unlearn.

It's easier to program than it is to deprogram.

Someone says, "You can't teach an old dog a new trick." I say, "Well, you can if the dog wants to learn it." We must unlearn what we have been taught so that God can give us the fresh bread of truth. After we unlearn, we must deprogram. God comes and cleans off the inner system of subtle programing that the world has downloaded inside of us. Then He reprograms us to His system of values and virtue.

It's a very sobering thought to see that we are programmed wrong. You've heard the old saying "go against the grain." I think we should "go against the soil the grain is planted in." The grain is not the problem, the dirt is. The soil of the soul has been plowed with the blades of modern society. How we think, who we are, and how we talk is all a result of the environment around us. This book is not written to get you to become a monk or live in a shell, but rather to open your eyes to the blueprint God has designed for you. God didn't design for you to live in a flowerpot, but He brought about your existence for a much deeper purpose. Get out of the flowerpot and get into the field!

THE JONESES MOVED

I hear people say, "I wish I had that house." I want to ask them "Do you want that debt too?" In the early chapters I wrote about the false concept of *keeping up with the Joneses*. Research confirms that the Joneses never paid their mortgage and were evicted. Further research indicates they relocated to the penitentiary, or possibly the state of regret. The Joneses are the invisible voice inside of your head saying "get, get, and get."

The most expensive place in the world is the graveyard. The reason is because most people die with God's blueprint laying untouched, unrolled, and unfulfilled. They worked for years to try to keep up with a crowd. The Joneses principle is not a biblical one. God doesn't want you examining your blueprint in the living room of others. Having things isn't evil. Having money isn't evil. The lust of money is what kills us. Money is like oxygen-it is a high necessity in order to exchange anything in this culture.

Instead of asking ourselves "What will make a lot of money?" We should be asking God "What makes me? What makes me what you want me to be?" *Follow the dream and not the green.* God will provide for you and go above and beyond all of your expectations.

To have and work a job is biblical. Scripture says "…ye walk worthy of the **vocation** wherewith ye are called." **Ephesians 4:1(b), King James Version**

Our definition of vocation is "trade or profession."

The definition of vocation in Ephesians 4 is "divine call."

You do the math here. God was and is saying that our divine calling and our trade overlap. We are NOT just Christians inside the church door and employees outside the church door.

DELAY

I ask myself on a weekly basis if I am living a life worthy of what God intended when He had me in mind. Am I giving Him all I have? More than anything, I don't want to die wrong. I don't mean dying in a spiritually lost state. I mean simply that I don't want to die out of God's will for my life, off the course He wanted me to run, and with unfulfilled blueprints. More than anything, I want to leave this world strong, not wrong.

Resting in God is a good thing but growing complacent is not!

Having confidence is a good thing, but arrogance is a sour aroma. Having God comfort me is a good thing, but pity is a powerless visitor. You see, we can receive comfort knowing that our sins are forgiven and that the love of God has been extended to us, but there's no room for complacency. When our love for Jesus grows cold so will our love for anything else. Sure, we may fill our lives with things that fill our flesh, but nothing will satisfy us.

I have to rest in God when I feel as though I'm not walking stride for stride with the Lord. The devil wants to destroy us all, but rarely comes with a red suit and pitchfork in hand. So many other "d's" are in the devil's arsenal of attack. He will come with distraction, discouragement, bad doctrine, and on and on. One "d" that he will use is our own delay. The Holy Spirit speaks to us and like a teenager who has been addressed by a parent, we have a mental delay in our responsiveness to Him. What happens next? Well, a thick heart toward God will put us a little off course with the Lord. Our position hasn't changed in Christ. We are still saved. However, our condition has weakened, and we are delayed by our own complacency.

SIX MONTHS TO LIVE

If you knew that you had six months, or less, to live, would you be arguing with people about foolishness? Would you be worrying about the things you are worried about right now? That answer is "no", I hope. You would prioritize your entire life at the highest level. Now, given, maybe you wouldn't fly to the mountains, or across the sea, but you would genuinely make all effort to place unimportant things aside and immerse yourself in the simple blessings of parents, children, or family in general.

I have witnessed some people also take the most precious last days of their life and serve the homeless, climb a mountain, or simply live out forgotten adventures. Still, if you knew you had days to live, you would prioritize at the highest level imaginable to make the most of the time you had left.

It doesn't matter what you do, if you don't do what you should do. Your calling from God matters and you will stand in account for what you did with the blueprints God gave you. Now, until we lay aside *our* agenda, we will never live out the blueprints God has for our life. Jesus knew that He would be crucified and just hours before that, He didn't call a meeting and weep with His circle of friends and talk about how great He was. He washed their feet. ***He served them.***

Selfish people don't serve.

They don't serve the Lord.
They don't serve their family.
They don't serve their neighbor.
They don't serve their generation.

Everything about selfish people centers around their own comfort and their own well-being.

They want to be served.

They want to get served.

They will critique the way you serve.

They have high standards of what it requires to please them.

But they will never serve WITHOUT a baited motive for later.

What good is all the stuff we have if we don't use it to serve a higher purpose? I don't want to be the god of my own world. That's a recipe for danger. In the life of a selfish person, you will find nothing that they submit to. They won't submit to anything bigger than themselves.

SMALL BOATS, BIG DREAMS

What bigger boat have you connected your vessel to? Are we like Simon Peter who looked at Jesus when he was told to throw his nets on the other side of the boat? Simon looked at Jesus and in so many words said "Hey, I'm the fisherman here. You stick to preaching." Peter went ahead and obliged him, and threw his net out thinking that he knew the net would come back empty. Boy, was he wrong! The nets immediately were engulfed with fish.

Imagine how many other fishermen ran from the shore wanting to buy Simon Peter's boat or rent his net?

Great things happen when we connect ourselves with people who have a greater authority in diverse areas that perhaps we don't. The real question is why wouldn't we? Why wouldn't we want to learn from those who have been there and done that. Sure, experience isn't everything in life, but certainly God will bring people into our life hoping we will attach our small vessel to theirs.

Someone else's boat doesn't have to be bigger in size to have great authority. I live near the great Savannah River Port. On a daily basis you can see small, yet powerful tug boats pulling and guiding massive vessels up the river and to the port. That massive vessel may need to empty its freight or be worked on, but either way, it submits to the smaller vessel.

Can you submit to what you see as smaller than you? I have and it's liberating.

We, as people, don't know it all. In fact, we only know in part. Furthermore, the part we know is very small.

God may be watching you to see if you will be a team player in a certain situation. Great leaders know how to be great followers. Nothing is original and it is wise, indeed, to connect with others who have watched their blueprints live, die, and live again.

Let God connect you with survivors, dreamers, workers, worshippers, and warriors. Attach your vessel to them and let others pull you along, as you are doing your part as well!

YOU CAN!

Discovering what you were designed to be and do in this life might not be as hard as you are thinking. Everything happens when you find your divine blueprints and really nothing happens until you do! This season of your life can be the most effective season you have ever experienced. Life can burst again for you in a sea of technicolor.

You can live again.
You can love again.
You can learn again.

You can!

Because God said you could.

Stop measuring yourself against the wins or losses of others.
Stop trying to outlive your past.
Stop judging yourself on what has happened in your life.

You can't run from the ghosts of yesteryear. I tried that too. Introduce the ghosts of yesteryear to Jesus and let Him fight those battles.

You can make it. I did. I came from nothing. No one knew me or had a greater prophetic revelation that my life was going to be anything even close to significant. If you could have seen my life, you would have said that the blueprints were in need of a do over. It's time for the colors of your life to burst in technicolor. You can't waste another moment as a prodigal meandering through life. More than anything, my heart pounds for you because I've been at life's lowest spots.

I wasn't the kid born with a silver spoon in my mouth, not even in my life. My silver spoon was more of a dirty wooden spoon. My life was not the envy of anyone. I don't want to give you the details in full of my life, but from my early adolescence through high school, life was the darkest shade of night that I could possibly describe to you. There were times I wanted to die. Literally.

I even prayed to God to take my life a few times as a struggling teenager. Life got dark. I felt that same darkness when Lindsey and I buried our daughter, Eva, in 2013. I've been at the bottom of life.

I tell you the truth about the bottom of life, God knows exactly where it's at. Yes indeed. Jesus Christ, the Prince of the Kings of the earth, holds the keys to death, hell, and the grave. He overcame. Jesus won the victory and the demonic voices that are shrieking inside of your heart-they fear His existence. They tremble at His very name. They want to keep you bound and tied to the patterns and prints of death and hopelessness, but Jesus has the keys to unlock the scroll to your blueprint. He won the right to lead you out of darkness and into His marvelous light. Give Him a chance, He died for the opportunity. Jesus won and so can you.

Everyone wants to get something. The cry of our day is "What's in it for me?" Everyone seems to be standing in an invisible line waiting to be the *next great thing*.

I don't want to die fully intoxicated on this life. I want to give it all away. I want to give my children clues, hints, and keys to their blueprint. I want to live in the center of God's will for my life. I want to win human souls for Christ. I want to leave this world, when it's my time, laying empty at the feet of Jesus, dead and yet, more alive than ever.

More than anything, I want to stand before the King of the Ages with peace in my heart, knowing nothing was held back.

The Lord has a package for you. He waits for you to sign off on it and receive it.

Open it.

It has *your blueprints.*

THE BOLDPRINT

> ## YOU CAN MAKE IT. I DID.

References

Bella, T. (2018, September 4). 'Just Do It': The surprising and origin story of Nike's slogan. *The Washington Post*. Retrieved from https://www.washingtonpost.com/news/morning-mix/wp/2018/09/04/from-lets-do-it-to-just-do-it-how-nike-adapted-gary-gilmores-last-words-before-excution/?noredirect

Cetas, A. (2009, January 21). The perfect sentence. *Our Daily Bread*. Retrieved from https://odb.org/2009/01/21/the-perfect-sentence/

Lehrer, J. (2012). 'How creativity works': It's all in your imagination. [online interview]. NPR. Retrieved from https://www.npr.org/2012/03/19/148777350/how-creativity-works-its-all-in-your-imagination

Sandler, A. (2011). *The Price is Right*. [Television Series]. Los Angeles, CA: CBS Television City.

Way, B. (2010, October 21). The world's largest puzzle. Retrieved from https://ezinarticles.com/?The-Worlds-Largest-Puzzle&id=5246946

Made in the USA
Columbia, SC
07 March 2020

88849710R00120